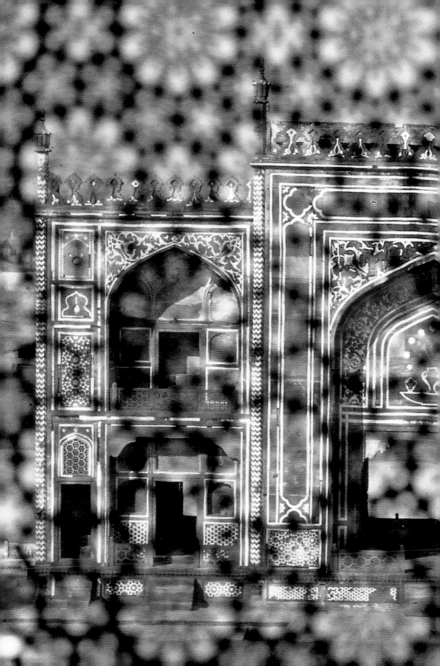

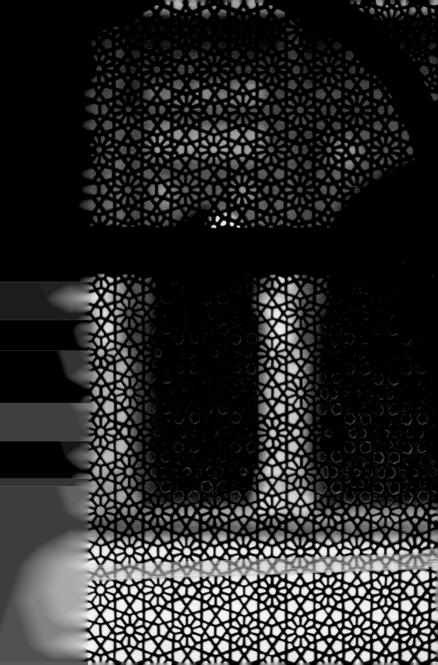

CONTENTS

INDIA AND
THE MUGHAL DYNASTY

Valérie Berinstain

DISCOVERIES®

HARRY N. ABRAMS, INC., PUBLISHERS

In 1526, when Babur, a Turko-Mongol prince from Central Asia, conquered Ibrahim Lodi, the sultan of Delhi, at the battle of Panipat, he realized the unfinished dream of his ancestor Timur: the submission of the Indian subcontinent. In his four-year reign he founded the Mughal dynasty that dominated India for more than three centuries.

CHAPTER 1

THE BEGINNING OF THE MUGHAL EMPIRE

The Mughal emperors constantly legitimized their power by stressing their lineage from Timur and Genghis Khan. This miniature (opposite) depicts Timur seated between his descendant Babur, to whom he is offering the crown of India, and Babur's son, Humayun.

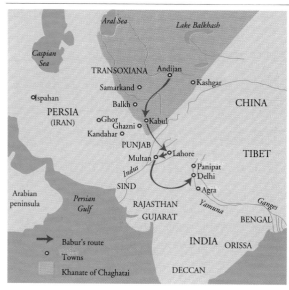

The khanate of Chaghatai, from which Babur originated, is located between the Aral Sea to the west, the Kashgar oasis to the east, and Afghanistan and Kashmir to the south. Below and opposite: details from a 15th-century painting depicting a Mongol nomad camp – a nomadism explaining the uncertainties of the first Mongol conquerors of India, victorious one moment, or wandering with a

Just before the Mughal conquest, at the beginning of the 16th century, India comprised a vast number of kingdoms, of varying power, ruled by Hindu or Muslim sovereigns, defenders of the two religions that had come to dominate since Buddhism had started to decline. As soon as Muslim expansion began in the 7th century, India was affected. Whereas the South was relatively stable – Tamil country was dominated by the Chola kingdom, while the Rashtrakutas controlled Maratha country – the North was the scene of rivalries between Hindu clans: the Guraja-Pratihara in the Kanauj region, several Rajput principalities in the Thar region, and the Shahi in the Punjab. After two years Arab generals succeeded in 713 in seizing the province that was most exposed to these invaders from the west: Sind. Moreover, the subcontinent and its riches encouraged numerous merchants from the Arabian peninsula to settle in Indian ports in order to trade. Tolerated by the Hindus, they played an active role in the spread of Islam in India.

few followers the next.

Central Asia, cradle of empires

From the 8th century the Islamization of Persia (now Iran) and the nomadic Turkish populations of Central Asia had reinforced Muslim power in this part of Asia. Under the yoke of the Muslim invaders, these Turkish tribes integrated the Arabo-Persian culture of their new masters. Skilled horsemen and good archers, they enlisted the troops of the armies of the caliphate of Baghdad, in which they played an increasing role. Some historians consider that, while administration remained in the hands of the Arabo-Persians, the military power of the Muslim world in this period passed to the Turks. The weakening of the Baghdad caliphate in the 10th century led a great number of these Turks to take their independence, especially in Central Asia, where they founded states whose princely courts and administrative systems were inspired by the Persian model, which was then the only one in force in the Muslim world. Under pressure from the advancing Mongol tribes, they turned to Persia where the Oghuz gave rise in the 11th century to the dynasty of the Seljuks. In the 13th century, one of them, Osman, founded the dynasty of the Osmanlis, the future Ottomans, in Asia Minor. Others turned towards India. The infighting that divided the Hindu clans and their clumsy military tactics certainly encouraged these

Among the nomads of Central Asia, a chief's prestige attracted minority clans and adventurers to join him. These tribes were constantly on the move, seeking pastures for their flocks. Excellent horsemen, they had to assert themselves with bows and spears. In the 6th and 7th centuries, the Turks, who originated in high Asia, emerged from the numerous peoples who crossed the steppes. In the 11th century they dominated Transoxiana, and at the end of the 12th, near Lake Baikal, the Mongol Genghis Khan imposed his authority and, in twenty years, built up an immense empire stretching from the Caspian Sea to northern China.

Central Asia is crossed by the Silk Road, which, since ancient times, has been a commercial network linking Europe and Asia.

Turkish tribes from Central Asia to seize India's riches under the pretext of a holy war (*jihad*).

The first Indian Muslim dynasties

At the beginning of the 11th century, a Turkish tribe originating in the town of Ghazni, led by Mahmud of Ghazni, annexed North India and, in 1022, founded the city of Lahore, the first Muslim Indian capital. At the end of the 12th century another chief, who came from Ghor, a small Central Asian principality located between Ghazni and Herat, decided in his turn to conquer the valley of the Ganges, which was subject to the Muslim power of the Ghaznevids, while another branch of the Turks who had settled in Kharezm took possession of Afghanistan.

In 1192 Muhammad of Ghor struck at the heart of India when Prith Viraj, the Rajput hero and symbol of Hindu resistance, fell under the assaults of his troops. After having destroyed the Hindu temples that he encountered on his path, the Turkish sultan established Muslim power in North India on a long-term basis. Having taken possession of Delhi, he made one of his slaves, Qutb ud-din-Aibak, a general and left him in charge of the city; then he departed again for Ghor. The first Indian Muslim dynasty, known as the Slave dynasty, emerged from this first group of conquerors. Still attached at that time to the caliphate of Baghdad, it finally achieved independence in 1258 when the latter was dissolved. After that, the Muslim sultans of India no

It was at the battle of Tarain, in 1192, north of Delhi, that the army of the Rajput Prith Viraj (left) was annihilated by the Muslims.

longer felt any ties to the Middle East, the cradle of Islam. The Slave dynasty (1210–90) was succeeded by the Khalji dynasty (1290–1320), Turkish dissidents who were then posted as governors of Bengal. It is characterized by the personality of the sultan Ala-ud-din.

The Tughluq dynasty, which superseded the Khalji in 1320, ushered in the start of Muslim domination in

Deogarh was already an important intellectual and artistic centre under the Hindu Yadava dynasty. The Bahmani fortified the site of Daulatabad (below), making it

southern India. In 1327 Muhammad ibn Tughluq (r. 1325–51) decided to move his capital from Delhi to the northern Deccan, and founded the city of Daulatabad on ancient Deogarh. Five years later he had to return to the North to repel a Mongol invasion, and abandoned his new capital.

Twenty years later, Daulatabad seceded, and the former general of the dynast, Ala-ud-din Bahman Shah, founded the Bahmani dynasty, which, for more than a century, controlled a large part of the Deccan, whose territories had, until then, been Hindu. At the end of the 15th century and the beginning of the 16th, this sultanate was divided into five kingdoms: Berar, Ahmednagar, Bidar, Golconda and Bijapur; the last two were the most renowned for their wealth.

impregnable. In 1633 it took Shah Jahan six months to seize the fort that is dominated by the Chand Minar.

After annexing a new territory, the Muslims erected mosques. At Delhi, that of Quwat al-Islam, dominated by the Qutb Minar (centre) was begun in the reign of Qutb ud-din-Aibak. Parts of destroyed Hindu and Jain temples were reused. Islam introduced the arch and mortar in India.

At the end of the 14th century, the Tughluq government fell prey to anarchy and could not stand up to the new expedition of Muslims from Central Asia led by the formidable Timur, the 'Lord of Iron', the great conqueror of eastern and western Persia.

The start of the Mughal dream

Timur, nicknamed Leng, 'The Lame' (hence the western deformation of his name to Tamerlane), was born in April 1336, at Kesh, to a family of the tribe of the Barlas, Turkized Mongols, who had joined Genghis Khan in the 13th century.

Timur's rise was dazzling. By 1370 he was in control of Transoxiana, had taken the title of great emir, and had made Samarkand his capital. In order to impose his authority over all the territories along the Silk Road, and to ensure the protection of his empire, he turned his attention to North India, which he intended to subdue. In 1398, after passing the Indus and conquering the town of Multan, his troops confronted the army of the ruler Mahmud Tughluq, sultan of Delhi. The victorious Timur entered the royal city, and his men laid it to waste. Before leaving again for Central Asia, taking with him to Samarkand the elephants and the best craftsmen of the city, he established a principle of

Following his marriage to a descendant of the great Khan, Timur gave himself the name *kurgan*, 'son-in-law'. It was his grandson, Ulug Beg, who asserted that his ancestor was a direct descendant of the great Genghis Khan, a link that Timur himself had never claimed. Above: one of the Mongol cavalrymen who made up Timur's army.

succession on the Tughluq sultanate, which he subsequently bequeathed to his grandson, the sultan Muhammad. It was this inheritance – quite theoretical when all is said and done, as Muhammad had never actually reigned over northern India – to which Babur laid claim when he conquered the subcontinent a century later.

The Lodi, last sultans of Delhi

The Tughluq never recovered from Timur's invasion. In 1414 they were overthrown by the Sayyids, dynasts of no great ability. Around 1450 the last Sayyid chose to withdraw to Budaun (to the east) and entrusted the sultanate to Bahlul Lodi, who became the first sultan of the dynasty with the same name in 1451. On his death in 1489, his son Sikandar Lodi was left with an explosive situation that he succeeded in mastering thanks to an efficient administration. In 1517 Ibrahim Lodi succeeded his father, and made a clumsy attempt to seize the kingdom of his brother Jaunpur, as a result of which the sultanate was split into two clans. This clumsiness was to be fatal to Ibrahim Lodi. His uncle, Alam Khan, who wanted to oust him, asked for help from Babur, who was just waiting for this chance to enter India. In 1524 he crossed the Indus with his soldiers and headed for Lahore to come to his aid. Once Lahore was conquered, Babur left for Kabul again.

Babur, a conqueror in search of an empire

Zahiruddin Muhammad Babur, a Chaghatai Turk, was born at Andijan in 1483. He was only eleven when he inherited Ferghana, a small province in Transoxiana. Valiant in combat, Babur, 'The Leopard', began by repelling the assaults by neighbouring lords who coveted

On the death of Genghis Khan (above) in 1227, the huge empire was divided between his four sons. One of them, Chaghatai, gave his own name to a collection of disparate provinces, and his name was also given to the language in use, eastern Turkish. In the 14th century, politico-religious disagreements split the khanate in two. The nomad tribes of animist tradition established themselves in Mongolia, while more sedentary populations, who converted to Islam, settled in Transoxiana, a province controlled by the Chaghatai lords who had seized power because of the weakening of Genghis Khan's authority. Babur was born in this province.

his modest province. He found that the best form of defence was attack. His ambition grew and he became obsessed by a single thought, that of carving out a real empire for himself and reigning over Samarkand. From then on he continually threw his troops into battle with a view to taking Timur's city.

Samarkand: the impossible dream

In 1497 Babur succeeded in taking Samarkand from his cousin Baisunghar Mirza. However, he entered a ravaged metropolis over which he would rule for only a hundred days. Three years later, he set off again to attack the city of his ancestors, now occupied by the Uzbeks. The Uzbek hordes had been opponents of the Timurids (descendants of Timur) since the 15th century, and were carving out a powerful state in Transoxiana. Their chief, Shaibani Khan, a skilful politician, tried every means at his disposal to oust the Timurids in order to reign over this part of Central Asia. Babur succeeded in forcing the Turquoise Gate and entering Samarkand, applauded by a jubilant crowd. It was just a respite. In the spring of 1501, the Uzbeks again decimated the armies of the young ruler – he was still only eighteen – and, after a long siege, he once again had to abandon the town. Babur therefore turned towards Afghanistan. In 1504 he succeeded in taking Kabul, where he consolidated his local power and took the title of padishah (a Persian word equivalent to the Arab term sultan). Located on a strategic commercial route, Kabul was a rich city. Caravaneers and merchants

Of his entry into Samarkand in 1500 (below), Babur wrote: 'The towns-people were still slumbering; a few traders peeped out of their shops, recognized me and put up prayers. When, a little later, the news spread through the town, there was rare delight and satisfaction for our men and the townsfolk. They killed the Auzbegs [Uzbeks] in the lanes and gullies with clubs and stones like mad dogs....'
Babur, *The Babur-nama in English (Memoirs of Babur)*, trans. Annette S. Beveridge, Vol I, 1922

from China, Persia, Iraq and India thronged there to sell cotton fabrics, crystallized sugar, horses and slaves.

For ten years, Babur divided his ambitions between Central Asia and India

Wearied by his conquests, the ruler appreciated the temperate climate of the Afghan city, where he devoted himself to hunting and to observing nature. He built the Garden of Fidelity, a real paradise on earth. Yet Babur remained ready to do anything to retake Samarkand. In 1511 he renounced his Sunni faith to gain the goodwill of an important ally, Ismail, shah of Persia, thereby reaffirming his opposition to the Uzbeks, who were fervent Sunnis. Supported by the Persian armies, he was victorious, but shortly afterwards the departure of the shah's armies prevented him from resisting an Uzbek offensive. His hopes of making Timur's empire rise from its ashes at Samarkand were dashed. From 1514 Babur abandoned his aims in Central Asia and devoted himself to the conquest of India. His successors in India all entertained the ambition of

Babur's features – light skin, slightly drawn-out black eyes, high cheekbones – underlined his origins in Central Asia (left).

Courageous in combat, Babur was the great conqueror of India, where he established one of the most important dynasties of the modern oriental world. Nevertheless his modesty and his simplicity led him to prefer wide open spaces and nature to the pomp of the court. A religious man, well-read and a poetry-lover, Babur translated legal and religious texts, and composed verses in Persian, a language he spoke perfectly and whose poetry he loved. From 1520 – in a very original undertaking for the period – he started to write his memoirs, probably from notes made every day for several years. In writing the *Babur-nama* in Chaghatai Turkish, his mother tongue, and not in Persian, which for a long time had been the cultural language of Central Asia, Babur intended to stress the originality of his clan among the numerous tribes of Central Asia.

The *Babur-nama* was valued by Babur's descendants. His grandson Akbar paid homage to him by having it translated into Persian and illustrated with numerous miniatures, since the original manuscript did not have any. At first sight, the memoirs seem to be a portrait of an introverted, frank man: shy, solitary and modest – modest in his triumphs, and modest with his soldiers, sharing their harsh existence during his campaigns. The three miniatures on the left, taken from the *Babur-nama*, illustrate the journey of Babur's armies to India. On leaving Herat to go to Kabul, they were overtaken by snow (opposite). Having reached a cave that was too narrow to accommodate all his soldiers, Babur decided to sleep outside with them: 'Some of my men in snow and storm, I in the comfort of a warm house! the whole horde (*aulus*) outside in misery and pain, I inside sleeping at ease! That would be far from a man's act, quite another matter than comradeship! Whatever hardship and wretchedness there is, I will face ... to die with friends is a nuptial.' (Trans. A. S. Beveridge, Vol I, 1922.)

reconquering the Timurid capital, which they considered the cradle of the Mughals.

In 1525 Babur, who was back in Central Asia, found himself once again called upon to help Alam Khan, on whom the sultan Ibrahim Lodi had just inflicted a bitter defeat. A few months later, Babur returned to North India at the head of a big army, but this time on his own behalf.

The elephants of Ibrahim Lodi and the cavalry of Babur's army face each other at the battle of Panipat (below and opposite, miniatures taken from the *Babur-nama*).

The battle of Panipat

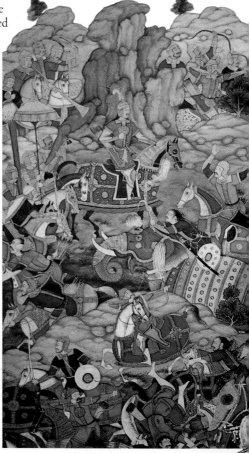

After having subdued Lahore once more, Babur and his army marched on the capital, Delhi, in order to subjugate the sultan Ibrahim Lodi once and for all. Humayun, Babur's son, foiled a first attack. On reaching the village of Panipat, in the plain north of Delhi, Babur organized his forces. He quickly noticed his inferiority in numbers: he had only 12,000 men, of whom about half were fit for attack. Hardened to war in the course of his numerous battles with the Uzbeks, and a skilful strategist, Babur knew that this time his enemies were very poor soldiers. Moreover, he had at his side two talented Turkish gunners who had mastered the art of war and cannons, a weapon unknown on the subcontinent. The order was given to tie all the carts together to form a large defensive circle, as was done in the country of *Rum* (Asia Minor). The men, protected by mantelet shields, horses and cannons, took up positions between the 700 carts. Ibrahim Lodi hesitated to fight despite his 100,000 men and his 1500 elephants. In order to incite the enemy to attack, Babur sent his soldiers by night to harass the guards. On the morning of 21 April 1526 the exasperated Lodi finally started to attack. He forced the right wing, but his army was swiftly overwhelmed by the cannon fire and the arquebuses set up in the centre. Terrorized by the noise of the cannons, the elephants bolted, making any attack impossible. At midday, Ibrahim Lodi's camp was destroyed. His remains were brought to Babur, who had him decapitated.

Very quickly Babur became preoccupied with protecting the treasures of Delhi and Agra from pillage by his victorious troops. He sent Humayun to Agra, and marched on Delhi, where he proclaimed himself padishah of Hindustan in the great mosque. On that day, more than a century after Timur, Babur was victorious. At Agra, the new conqueror of India was greeted by his son, who presented him with a magnificent diamond, probably the Kohinur (now part of the British crown jewels), of which it was said at the time that its value would provide

At the beginning of the 16th century firearms were not much used in India. Soldiers preferred the bow or sabre, so an army's elite corps was made up of archers. Babur, who took advice from Turkish artillerymen, was interested in firearms and especially cannons, which were more effective than the culverins and arquebuses of the past. He supervised the casting of pieces and attended firing practices.

'two and a half days' food for the whole world'. Babur immediately refused this rich gift, and offered it to the one who wanted to give it to him, Humayun.

After hesitating, Babur decides to remain in India

From then on, Babur laid the foundations of a new dynasty, soon to be called by the name of 'Mughal', a Persian word designating these new-comers from the North, the country of the Mongols. Babur's reign was short-lived – just four years, during which he strove to consolidate effective control over the conquered territory, by enlarging it but also, and especially, by subduing any rebellions that arose. While a great number of Indian Muslim kingdoms submitted to the new conquerors, the defenders of Hinduism, especially the Rajputs of Rajasthan, rose up in revolt. The confederacy led by Rana Sanga of Mewar was very soon subjected to the assaults of the new masters of northern India, who conquered Chitor, Kanua and Chandiri in 1528, and then, the following year, suppressed the rebellion of the Afghans of Bihar, winning a decisive victory that consolidated their power for a long time.

Despite the goodness that his contemporaries ascribed to him, Babur had to punish his enemies to assert his power. Although he declared holy war against 'infidels', he took no oppressive action against Hindus. He even went as far as visiting their temples, whose lack of symmetry and excessive decoration he disliked (above, Babur with Hindu ascetics).

'Hindustan is a country of few charms'

Despite his rapid rise and the extent of his empire, which included Afghanistan, Kashmir and the Punjab to the north, Bihar to the east and Malwa to the south-west, Babur did not like India and was full of nostalgia for the mountains of Central Asia. He was distressed to note that there were no running-waters in Indian gardens.

In his new capital of Agra – Delhi symbolized the fallen power of the old Muslim dynasties – he had gardens constructed, notably the Garden of the Eight Paradises, where he liked to spend time between two conquests, just as he had at Kabul, in the Garden of Fidelity.

An empire with feet of clay

Babur was, above all, a warrior, not an administrator or a manager. Although he consolidated the territorial foundations of his new empire, he did not undertake any administrative reforms. The immense territories that then comprised his kingdom were always organized according to the system of 'provinces' (*pargana*) put in place by the preceding Muslim dynasties. Each of them was controlled by a kind of governor who, being answerable only to the central power, often acted like a despot over the local populations. He had to collect the taxes on his lands, and then turn them over to the central power after having deducted his expenses, and he was obliged to maintain an army to reinforce the sultan's when the need arose. In reality this system favoured the independence of the provinces, which regularly rebelled against the dynast by threatening to secede. The setting up of a political and economic administration would have enabled Babur to affirm his central power and to channel the money properly – money which he spent heedlessly, squandering most of it.

In March 1527, two days before his battle against the confederacy led by Rana Sanga, Babur (centre opposite), gave up wine to obtain God's favour. Thanks to his cannons and his cavalry, which was far more mobile than the Rajput elephants, he decimated his adversaries. Later Babur wrote in his memoirs: 'In truth the longing and craving for a wine-party has been infinite and endless for two years past, so much so that sometimes the craving for wine brought me to the verge of tears. Thank God! this year that trouble has passed from my mind, perhaps by virtue of the blessing and sustainment of versifying the translation.' (Trans. A. S. Beveridge, 1922.)

Above: the ramparts of the Rajput fortress of Gwalior.

فرمودم كه اين جى ابر جه وپـــياق ساخـتـذليسارهى خالى

The pre-Islamic Orient already attached great importance to gardens, which, through their abundance of water and vegetation, symbolized places of well-being in an arid world. Thus was born Paradise, *Pairi-daeza* (which in Persian means 'closed walled garden'). Mindful of his nomadic origins, Timur rarely resided inside buildings, and preferred to set up court in vast cloth encampments which he had erected within orchard-gardens. These gardens corresponded to the plan of the *chahar bagh*, or 'garden in four parts'. Within a quadrangular enclosure, two water-courses crossed at their mid-point to divide the space into four parts, themselves sometimes redivided into four. Symbolizing the four parts of the world, these beds were planted with fruit trees and various plants among which the rose ruled supreme. This plan became classic and spread throughout both Muslim and Rajput India. Babur had a good many gardens constructed in Central Asia and in India. The best known is the Garden of Fidelity at Kabul (opposite). Left: Babur supervising the gardeners' work.

The treasure that was amassed in the course of this conquest of India was used for generous distributions to both his allies and the religious figures who were the guarantors of the new state's Islamic character. And yet, even though the emperor presented himself as a Muslim ruler, appointed by God and omnipotent, he was far from being a fanatic and displayed a certain tolerance towards non-Muslims. His Central Asian origins probably favoured this open-mindedness, since Central Asia had always been a meeting place of different cultures, religions and ways of thinking from both East and West. In October 1530 Humayun fell ill. While all the doctors believed that he would die very soon, it was in fact Babur who passed away.

Humayun: an interrupted reign

Born in Kabul in 1508, Humayun, 'The Lucky', became emperor at the age of twenty-three, succeeding his father as head of a vast but fragile empire. Before this accession to power, which aroused widespread opposition, the young prince had fought at his father's side and had even tried to realize Babur's dream by setting off to conquer Samarkand before he fell ill. The young monarch was particularly good and lenient, and respected the Turko-Mongol tradition of his ancestors, sharing power with his three half-brothers. He was

Open to the Indian Ocean and its maritime trade, the rich province of Gujarat is an important region for the economy of north-west India. Apart from its numerous ports, it is also the point of embarkation for Muslim pilgrims to Mecca. Annexed to the sultanate of Delhi in 1297, it proclaimed its independence in 1401, in the reign of a Rajput who had converted to Islam. A fanatic, he had numerous Hindu temples destroyed, and erected mosques on their ruins. His son, Ahmad Shah (r. 1411–41), the real founder of this state, had a capital built, Ahmedabad, which he endowed with various monuments and mosques, the most famous of which is the *Jami Masjid* (below, detail of a *jali*).

the padishah, and these three were his vassals: Kamran was installed in Kabul and the Punjab, while Askari and Hindal possessed *jagirs* (revenue) from the north-east region of Delhi.

The empire was still under threat: Afghans, Rajput and Indian sultans redoubled their attacks when they perceived the Mughal weakness and lack of cohesion. Gujarat seceded, and its sultan, Bahadur Shah (r. 1526–37), turned to the Portuguese for help in fighting the Mughals. It was a waste of effort. Beaten, he had to take refuge at Diu, then under Portuguese domination, while Humayun seized his capital, Ahmedabad. He installed his half-brother Askari there, but, being incapable of stamping his authority on the various factions, Askari fled, thus depriving the Mughal empire of this rich province. To the east, in Bihar and Bengal, the emperor had to confront a formidable enemy, the Afghan Sher Shah, whose father had served the Lodi dynasty while he himself had been enlisted in Babur's armies. Since he did not get on with the Turks, he entered the service of an Afghan chief, and took advantage of Humayun's campaigns towards the west to seize Bengal. The worried padishah decided to reduce this new opposition force. He pursued the enemy as far as Gaur, the Bengali Muslim capital, while Sher Shah circumvented the Mughal army. The indecisive emperor waited several months before counter-attacking; and when at last he committed himself to battle, the monsoon slowed the movement of his armies, which became

In 1520 Babur (opposite) gave his eldest and favourite son, Humayun, the province of Badakshan. Although a poor warrior, Humayun was nevertheless at his father's side in all battles. On hearing of his son's illness, Babur was overwhelmed with grief. According to legend, he gave his life to save the one whom he had designated his successor.

Elegant in stature and dark-skinned, Humayun (left) liked to surround himself with learned people whom he received on Thursdays, the day of the planet Jupiter which belongs to scholars and nobles. Profoundly religious, and a follower of the Sunna, he was extremely tolerant. Unfortunately, his penchant for opium was detrimental to his public standing.

caught in the mud. Beaten a first time, Humayun wanted to attack again in 1540, but he suffered a bitter defeat at Kanauj and had to abandon the north of India to the Afghan clan.

Humayun's exile and the Afghan interlude of Sher Shah (r. 1540–5)

Threatened and betrayed by a large number of his officers when he tried to take refuge in Lahore, Humayun left India furtively by the north-west, crossed Sind and Afghanistan, and reached Persia. He abandoned everything to the new Afghan dynasty, except for the diamond his father gave him after the battle of Panipat. The young ruler of Persia, Shah Tahmasp, who at this time saw India as a possible escape route to the east from the threats of the Turks in Asia Minor and the Uzbeks offered the monarch asylum and soldiers to help him reconquer his empire. In exchange, he asked him to embrace Shiism, to give him the diamond, and to surrender Kandahar to him. The city was then in the hands of Kamran, Humayun's brother. Humayun accepted the first two conditions, but kept Kandahar once it had been taken from his brother, whom he ordered to be blinded and sent to Mecca.

While the Mughal was in exile, Sher Shah organized himself. He settled in Delhi, where he expanded the sixth city, Din Panah, which Humayun had hurriedly built in 1533. He conquered Agra and Lahore, and protected the province of Punjab with a line of fortifications. Having understood the risk posed by a division of power, he centralized it around his person. There was a succession of reforms: a reform of the agrarian system whereby the peasants were assured of his protection against any excesses by civil servants responsible for levying tax by having it fixed at a quarter or a third of harvests; a reform of the loan system whereby he incited farmers to acquire new lands in order to increase cultivation; and a reform of the armies, of which he demanded iron discipline. Large numbers of

Built in 1540 in the centre of an artificial lake, the tomb of Sher Shah (below) presages the monumental funerary art of the Mughal dynasts. During the first Indian sultanates, mausolea were more modest in size. The first, built in Delhi, were square in plan and topped by a dome. Moving from a square to a circular plan, they evolved towards a polygonal one, like the tomb of Sher Shah, which is embellished with numerous canopied

pavilions. In Islam, the presence of water is supposed to permit the deceased to quench his thirst before reaching Paradise.

troops were quartered in strategic points of the empire, inside formidable fortresses. For military but also commercial purposes he organized the construction of a network of roads linking the Punjab with Bengal and the city of Agra with Burhanpur and Rajasthan.

The successor of Shah Ismail, founder of the Safavid dynasty, Shah Tahmasp (r. 1524–76, left) pursued his father's politics to strengthen his power by defeating the Ottomans and the Uzbeks, his two main enemies. The young shah was also a fine scholar. A calligrapher of renown, and a lover of painting, he brought artists who were trained in the Timurid tradition to his new residence at Tabriz. Faced with the religious orthodoxy of the Safavid rulers, many nobles left Persia to seek refuge at the Mughal court.

With its scattering of caravanserais, this network facilitated trade between the provinces. Sher Shah unified the monetary system and, like every Muslim ruler, confirmed his adherence to Islam by minting coinage. Moreover, he was happy to marry Rajput princesses to establish links with the powerful rebel rajahs. In so doing, he laid the foundations for the changes that the emperor Akbar later made.

When Humayun reconquers his empire

In 1545 the death of Sher Shah ended the reign of a great sovereign. His sons and heirs did not have their father's genius, and could not check the multiple troubles that destabilized the kingdom: rebellions, intrigues.... Humayun had now settled in Kabul and having at last followed Babur's advice – 'govern by the sword and not by the pen' – he was awaiting an opportune moment to have his new army march on Lahore in order to finish once and for all with the Afghans who were settled in India. Once Lahore was conquered, the road to Delhi lay open to him. In July 1555 the exiled ruler entered the city.

In order to place Mughal power on the throne of India for good, he had to confront several threats – on the one hand, in the Punjab where the rebels were rapidly brought to heel by his general Bairam Khan, and, on the other, in the eastern regions where a certain Qambar Beg revolted, along with some adventurers who wanted to destroy Mughal power so as to share out its remains. The rebellion was shortlived, and Humayun's armies brought Qambar Beg's head back to Delhi. These would be the emperor's last victories before his death.

The Mughal empire by then comprised Afghanistan and the Punjab in the extreme north-west, the Delhi plain as far as Allahabad, and the Himalayan foothills to the east. However, as no reforms had been undertaken to consolidate Mughal power, it remained embryonic. Its revenues still depended on provincial governors responsible for collecting them from the district chiefs (*jagirdars*) who themselves levied them from the peasants. Famines had decimated the population, and money was lacking.

Moreover, the absence of a common language, the diversity of races and the multiplicity of cultures favoured the emergence of hotbeds of rebellion that constantly threatened the empire. Its only force resided in its army which had to impose its authority by eliminating

Following the advice of astrologers, Humayun had chosen the ancient site of Indraprastha, near Delhi, which was associated with the *Mahabharata*, to build his new capital, Din Panah. On his return from exile, he added to the city that Sher Shah had already completed an octagonal pavilion in the tradition of the Timurid garden pavilions (below). He is thought to have died in this building, which became his library. Passionately interested in astronomy, Humayun had seven audience chambers (durbars) built, each bearing the name of seven planets, where he could receive different people.

the principal opponents, the Afghan clan.

An intellectual and patron of the arts

An enlightened lover of art and literature, a calligrapher and poet, Humayun had kept in contact with Persian culture during his exile. Whereas Shah Tahmasp, as he grew old, turned away from the arts to take refuge in an austere life devoted to Islam, Humayun proposed to several artists that they should come and work for him at Kabul. Once back in his capital, he undertook, thanks to the painter Mir Sayyid Ali and the calligrapher Abd us-Samad, the founding of the first school of Mughal painting, which was later to shine with splendour. This first production was dominated by the Persian style, but became more liberated in Akbar's reign.

Humayun also devoted a great deal of his time to the study of astronomy, geography and mathematics, and he spent long periods observing the stars – a passion that was to prove fatal. The story goes that, one evening in January 1556, while he was observing Venus, he was taken by surprise by the call to prayer; wishing to kneel down to honour God, he caught his feet in the folds of his garment, and fell to the bottom of his library staircase, breaking his skull. Less than six months after the emperor's return from exile, the Mughal dynasty was weakened once again.

The few miniatures executed in the reign of Humayun still display Persian influence. Highly stylized, the pictures show three-quarters of the ovoid faces. The eyes are small, contrary to the Jain and Hindu pictorial tradition. Above: a painting depicting a young scribe, attributed to Mir Sayyid Ali.

Akbar's accession to power in 1556 marked a turning point in the history of the Mughal dynasty. By abandoning the custom of sharing power and by affirming his independence from the Islamic principles of sovereignty, he put in place a political, military and religious system that he controlled. His open-mindedness and tolerance held the empire together for one century.

CHAPTER 2

AKBAR THE GREAT

In having his new capital built at Fatehpur Sikri, Akbar broke away from the Mughal tradition that the emperor should reign at Agra or Delhi. By borrowing from Indian architecture, the new palatine city (left, its construction) reflected the personality of its sovereign who wanted above all to be a Muslim dynast in India.

Born on 15 October 1542 in the fort of Umarkot, on the edge of the Thar desert, Akbar spent his childhood being tossed this way and that by the conquests and misfortunes of his father, who nevertheless took great care to give him a solid education, rounded off by a rigorous physical training. Akbar was an excellent wrestler and a skilled horseman, but he encountered some difficulties in his studies. In 1554 it was as an accomplished warrior that he set out at his father's side to conquer India. No one could have then foreseen Humayun's tragic end two years later.

A child of thirteen ascends the throne

The prince learned of his father's death while he was fighting the Afghans again, and went down to Delhi. Recognized as the only heir to the Mughal crown, Akbar was proclaimed padishah at the age of thirteen. Too young to hold the reins of power by himself, the new ruler was assisted by Humayun's faithful companion in exile, Bairam Khan. The latter, having imposed the young dynasty on the Mughal armies, helped him to consolidate the frontiers left by Humayun and to smother the Afghan threats that, once again, hung over the embryonic empire. To the east, the danger came from a Hindu general by the name of Hemu who had gone over to the service of the Afghans and dreamed of overturning the Mughal ruler in order to re-establish Hindu domination in North India.

The Mughal forces defeated his army at Delhi, where Hemu was captured and executed. Sikandar Shah Sur, entrenched in the Punjab, constituted the other serious threat to the young Akbar. However, in 1557, having lost all support, the Afghan chief was compelled to surrender. He died two years later. Now that the Afghan threat was destroyed, Humayun's heritage was saved. The emperor concentrated on fortifying his empire.

In the fort of Umarkot a stela commemorates the birthplace of the 'Conqueror and Refuge of the World', Jalal ud-Din Mohammed Akbar Ghazi (above left).

During a tournament organized by Bairam Khan, the young Akbar proved his skill at shooting, which earned him a place at his father's side during his reconquest of India (above and detail opposite).

Bairam Khan, a burdensome regent

By turns soldier, tutor and dispenser of justice, Bairam Khan, a Shiite Turkoman of noble descent, was present on all fronts. His fame was established when the emperor blessed his marriage to his cousin Salima (daughter of Humayun's sister), not realizing that he was thus strengthening his tutor's grip on imperial power. The fits of temper, and the violence and ambition of Bairam Khan, so free with his advice and warnings, soon began to irritate Akbar, who felt his power was declining to the benefit of his *vakil* (prime minister). The latter was increasingly flaunting his Shiite sympathies, whereas the emperor defended the Sunni convictions of his Turkish ancestors. At the same time Akbar was under the influence of his nurse, Maham Anaga, who, despite her affection for the dynasty, was seeking to glorify her own son, the ruler's foster brother. In 1561, after an abortive attempt at rebellion, Bairam Khan was sent on a pilgrimage to Mecca. He was assassinated on the way. Some time later, Maham Anaga died in her turn. Hard hit by the loss of two beloved people, Akbar was at the same time relieved of the burden of their influence. He was now nineteen, and his reign could begin properly.

Since he always had in mind the image of his father, roaming without any kingdom, Akbar

Bairam Khan, who was appointed Akbar's tutor shortly before Humayun's death, found the young prince a Persian teacher called Mir Abdul Latif, who introduced him to the Sufi principle of *sulh i kull*, 'universal tolerance'. It had a decisive influence on Akbar's politics and religion.

undertook not only the consolidation of his empire's frontiers, but also the expansion of his territory. One of his first ambitions was to subjugate those notorious Rajput princes who regularly endangered the empire.

Rajasthan, bastion of Hindu resistance

In the 7th century this region, located in the north-west of the subcontinent, saw the emergence of kingdoms that were born of the disintegration King Harsha's empire. A great number of them were controlled by Rajput rulers, who claimed descent from the first Aryans to settle in India, though it is probable that some of them descended from a later set of invaders, the Gurjara, who came to India with the hordes of Hephtalite Huns in the 6th century.

In the 12th century the supremacy established by the Rajputs over a large part of North India was destroyed by the Muslim incursions. Rajput power was weakened at Tarain in 1192, and it was not until the 16th century and the destruction of the Delhi sultanate that it was restored, especially under the leadership of the successive rulers of Mewar. So Akbar decided to attack those behind the bellicose Rajputs, fervent defenders of Hinduism, the rajah of Mewar, whose capital, Chitor, located in the heart of Rajasthan, was protected by formidable ramparts.

On 20 October 1567 the Great Mughal and his army encircled the fortress that was reputed to be impregnable. He set out his cannons before starting to attack. Victory took a long time to achieve, and it was only in 1568 that the Mughal soldiers penetrated the Rajput bastion. The Hindus then rushed into bloody hand-to-hand fighting. In the face of his enemies' stubbornness, Akbar ordered the massacre of the population. Women and children had their throats cut unless they threw themselves into the flames to escape the enemy, in accordance with Rajput tradition…. Despite his victory, Akbar was filled with repugnance for

The last great Rajput fortress, Ranthambor, surrenders at the end of a short siege in 1569 (above).

this extreme violence. However, affairs of state compelled him; and after pillaging Chitor, Akbar subdued the other Rajput fortresses.

To subjugate the Rajputs once and for all, Akbar resorts to 'matrimonial diplomacy'

To smooth his relations with the Rajputs and to make allies of them, Akbar committed himself to matrimonial politics – a road already opened up by the Afghan Sher Shah – and married several Rajput princesses. He invited certain rajahs to court to be educated and trained in combat there, with the intention of serving in the armies of the Great Mughal. Some of them, fearing his superiority, submitted and entered his service. This sometimes stormy alliance was to be the strength of the Mughal empire.

In 1562 Akbar married the daughter of the rajah of Amber, Maryam Zamani, who gave birth to the future emperor Jahangir (below). The blood of the Rajputs was henceforth united with that of the Mughals. Secluded behind the walls of the imperial harem, the Rajput princesses were authorized to practise their cult in a little temple built for their use inside their apartments.

The surrender of the last northern Muslim kingdoms: when Akbar subdues Gujarat...

While Akbar achieved his conquests in Rajasthan, he harboured a feeling of distrust towards the independent kingdoms of Gujarat and Bengal.

Gujarat, profoundly shaken by Humayun's short-lived domination, was again weakened by internal quarrels that served the ambitions of the Portuguese. They had been in India since the end of the 15th century and seemed to want to expand their possessions in this part of the subcontinent. Akbar took advantage of the call for help from one of the sultans, Itimad Khan, who was anxious to supplant the other pretenders to power, to re-unite Gujarat to the Mughal empire. He also saw the opportunity to eliminate his relations in the Mirza clan who, following Turko-Mongol tradition, were demanding their share of power. At the end of an exhausting war of several months, the ruler succeeded in annexing Gujarat. He very rapidly boosted its economic situation: to facilitate the flow of its merchandise across the empire, he opened the road to Delhi and the far north to the Gujarati towns by perfecting the road network established by the Afghan Sher Shah.

The fort of Surat, the great Gujarat port, was built in 1540 to resist Portuguese attacks. It subsequently became the refuge of the Mirzas, Akbar's cousins. After several weeks of battle, Akbar entered the fortress in 1573 (above). To celebrate this victory he organized a great banquet during which, wanting to show his contempt for death, he almost impaled himself on a sabre while under the influence of alcohol.

...and then Bengal, Kashmir and Afghanistan

The province of Bengal was still under the domination of the Sur dynasty, and had always remained separate from the empire. In order to avoid any conflict, the sultan Suleiman Karanani for a long time showed allegiance to Mughal power. But his son Daud, thinking he might profit from the weakening of Akbar's armies, which were then at war in Gujarat, decided to overthrow him. Akbar dispatched one of his governors to Daud to reach a compromise. While his prime minister was ready to surrender, Daud had him assassinated, making the Great Mughal even more annoyed. Akbar then decided to be done with the sultan once and for all. In September 1574 victory was won, and Bengal was integrated into the empire.

Victorious on all fronts, the emperor regularly had to make sure that he had the support of his governors, and to repress any attempt at usurpation or desire for independence on the part of the subjugated kingdoms. In 1585 the unrest engendered by the Uzbeks at Kabul encouraged him to travel to the provinces of the far north of the empire, where all of the dignitaries assured him of their support. Having settled in

Angered by the opposition of Daud, son of the sultan of Bengal, Akbar had some boats fitted out to transport soldiers and horses to Patna by sailing up the Yamuna and the Ganges. In September 1574, after his defeat, Daud managed to flee to Orissa. It took the Mughal armies another two years to overcome the rebel ruler, who finally surrendered in July 1576 (below).

the Punjab, Akbar turned to Kashmir, whose ruler had always shown a certain resistance towards Mughal power. He proposed that this ruler should come and pay him homage. In view of the ruler's hesitation, the emperor decided to conquer this province.

Finally Akbar took advantage of the threats posed by the Uzbeks to the city of Kandahar to offer his help to the Persian governor, who accepted. However, once victory was won, Kandahar returned to the Mughal bosom in 1595. Fired by these successes, the emperor, a proud descendant of Timur, in his turn nurtured the idea of conquering Samarkand…. His dream was not to become reality, because he was called to other fronts.

The mirage of the Deccan

As the North of India was now under complete Mughal domination, Akbar turned to the South, renowned for its riches. Since the creation of the Bahmani kingdom in 1347, the Deccan had been coveted by the peoples of the North. However, the differences and quarrels that opposed Muslims, Indians and foreigners – Turks, Persians, Afghans – led to its break-up into five kingdoms, the two jewels of which were Bijapur, created in 1490, which dominated south-west India, and Golconda, founded in 1512, and located farther east. Constantly in contact with Persia through trade, especially in

The sultans of the Deccan were not very warlike, and appreciated the pleasures of the court. Aesthetes and patrons of the arts, they liked music and poetry. Although their studios rivalled Akbar's, the themes of their miniature paintings were different. Instead of official painting, the sultans preferred an intimate style that showed them reading, writing or resting.
Below: Ibrahim Adil Shah I, sultan of Bijapur.

horses, these two kingdoms were under Shiite rule, while Bidar, Ahmednagar and Berar upheld Sunnism. Religious differences and territorial ambitions created constant friction between these five Muslim states, though they nevertheless succeeded in forming an alliance in 1565 to annihilate the expansion plans of their Hindu neighbour, the empire of Vijayanagar, which controlled the far south of the subcontinent.

In 1599, after the towns of Ahmednagar and Asirgarh had fallen, the imperial troops set off on the road to the Deccan. Feeling threatened, the Muslim sultans of Bidar, Golconda and Bijapur sent missions to the Great Mughal to propose peace. However, destiny was to decree otherwise: taking advantage of the absence of his father Akbar, who was busy waging war in the Deccan, the

At the start of the 16th century the sultans of the Qutb Shahi dynasty (1512–87) transformed the fort of Golconda into a prosperous city. The palace, originally encircled by several ramparts, is now mere ruins (above).

young prince Salim (the future emperor Jahangir) had himself declared king at Allahabad. When Akbar was notified, he quickly returned to his capital, totally abandoning his aspirations in the Deccan....

The centralization of power

Since his childhood, the emperor had remembered just one lesson: power must not be shared. Akbar inaugurated a new era characterized by the desire to centralize everything around himself. Henceforth, he alone was entitled to make and unmake the fortunes of some people, so that nobody would turn a sword on the padishah. As Akbar had understood that executive power must not be left in the hands of the prime minister (*vakil*) alone, he decided to share the responsibility for the empire's main areas of administration (finance, army, justice and religion, royal household) among four different ministers.

From 1572 he undertook an important series of reforms, the main aim of which was to increase the revenues of the central state. He divided the empire into twelve provinces (*suba*) and appointed as the head of each a governor whose duty was to administer its territory, with the help of a *diwan* to collect the taxes and a *sadr* to look after religion. The governor no longer collected taxes directly, but was remunerated by the central authority, according to his rank and his responsibility (*mansab*), which was not hereditary (nor were any titles). If this civil servant

From 1590 to 1595, at Akbar's request, Abul Fazl wrote two chronicles of his reign: The *Akbar-nama*, and the *Ain-i-Akbari*, which

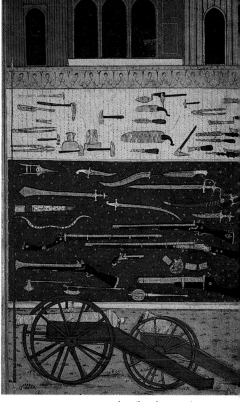

describes the organization of the imperial house.

died or was dismissed, the *suba* returned to the emperor who would appoint someone else at its head. In order to avoid the formation of excessively powerful local authorities, these administrators, of different religions and ethnic origins, were regularly transferred.

Having noticed that the diversity of languages and cultures caused discord, Akbar imposed Persian as the court's official language. Yet he also re-adopted the method of government that was in force in every Muslim state, whether Persian or Arabic, and adapted it to his own needs: to counter the doctors of Islam who reproached him for his lack of firmness and of respect for Koranic law, he even abolished Islam as the state religion. Similarly, so that the calendar of harvests and that of tax-levies would correspond to India's seasons, he replaced the Muslim era of Hegira with the *ilahi* era, of Persian type, whose months bore Zoroastrian names.

Finally, to facilitate commercial trade, Akbar improved the road network that had been set in place by Sher Shah by installing customs posts and by making it safer, so that merchandise could move around India and reach the ports to be exported. He also reformed the monetary system and replaced the old rupee with a new square one of silver, the *jalali rupiya*.

A whole chapter is devoted to the soldiers, another to the animals of war, and one to weapons (opposite). Another mentions the

jewels and precious stones in the treasury (above).

Architecture in the image of Mughal power

As soon as he had established his power and his authority was recognized by everyone, Akbar paid homage to his father by having a monumental tomb built, near Humayun's capital of Delhi. Begun in 1562, and completed in 1570, this mausoleum is a synthesis of Persian and Indian architecture. It also illustrates Akbar's wish to reveal the greatness of the Mughal empire through this monumental new architecture. While the tombs built under the sultanates of Delhi had a simple square plan, topped by a dome, and were made out of not very sturdy materials, Akbar chose to use more resistant materials, red sandstone and white marble, and to enhance the tomb by standing it on a vast terrace pierced with niches.

The monumentality of Humayun's tomb (below) marks a break with the architecture of the sultanates. Square in plan, the mausoleum is composed of five chambers in a quincunx, and four great points of entry. Probably the work of two stone-cutters from Central Asia, this architecture harks back to the Timurid edifices. The bulbous dome evokes those at Samarkand, the four turrets with little pavilions, *chhatri*, are of Indian inspiration; while the use of the red sandstone with inlaid white marble is peculiar to Muslim India.

Although insisting on his attachment to Islam, Akbar never undertook any holy war (*jihad*) against the infidels of India, and constructed a very limited number of mosques, buildings that generally symbolize the domination of a country by Muslims. Most of the mosques built in Akbar's reign adopt the plan of those built by the Indian sultans of previous periods: arcades surround a vast quadrangular court in the centre of which was a basin for ablutions. The direction of Mecca (*qibla*) is indicated by a niche in the wall (*iwan*) of a building at the west side. To this initial layout Akbar added a monumental gateway (*pistaq*) which not only gave access to the inner court, but also indicated the presence of a mosque to passers-by.

The most beautiful creation of this type is the mosque of his new capital at Fatehpur Sikri.

Opposite top: the monumental gateway (*pistaq*) of the mosque of Fatehpur Sikri.

Above: the construction of Fatehpur Sikri.

The very conception of the tomb comes from the religious ideology of the Mughal rulers. By building the mausoleum in the centre of a garden, *chahar bagh*, Akbar paid homage to his father, whom he thus designated as the master of the world.

Fatehpur Sikri, the 'City of Victory'

Having just had an immense red sandstone fort, Lal Qila, built in his capital at Agra, the emperor undertook in 1571 the construction of a palatine city on the site of a village called Fatehpur, where his grandfather Babur had once built a Garden of Victory. Fatehpur is located half-way between Agra and Ajmer, and the dynast often visited it during the pilgrimages he made to Ajmer to converse with a Sufi saint of the congregation of the

In the 13th century India's Muslim conquerors introduced the Sufi sect of the Chistis, which was very prominent in Afghanistan. Its first great representative, Muinuddin Chisti, died in 1233 at Ajmer, which became a Mecca for pilgrimage among the

Chisti. One day, when the emperor was despairing of ever having a son, the saint told him that a successor would soon be born. After this prediction miraculously came true in 1569 with the birth of Prince Salim, Akbar decided to leave Agra, which evoked too many family dramas for him, and set up his court at Fatehpur Sikri. In choosing this place for the establishment of his new capital, he also intended to break with the reigns of his predecessors, whose seats of power were either in Delhi or in Agra.

Indian Muslims. Akbar often went there until 1568, the year he began visiting a living saint, Salim Chisti, who lived at Fatehpur. In 1580 he had his mausoleum built in the courtyard of the Fatehpur mosque: a pavilion of white marble topped by a dome and surrounded by a closed corridor of *jali* (right).

This new palatine city took the form of a vast quadrilateral fortified on three sides and protected on the fourth by a hill. On the far north-east side stood the main entrance, a monumental gate (*Agra Darwaza*) to which the road from Agra led. All of the buildings built of red sandstone were set out according to a particularly complex urban plan, adapted to the site's topography, with a confusion of inner courtyards and buildings. The royal pavilions were erected on the

The public audience chamber, *diwan-i am* (1), marks the entrance to the imperial domain. On a vast terrace (2) stands the astonishing pavilion of private audiences, *diwan-i khass* (3), a small square building comprising two levels, separated on the outside by a balcony, and crowned by four *chhatri*. Further south, dominated by the *panch mahal* (4 and opposite in background), whose function remains an enigma, an immense pool (*anup talab*) (5 and opposite), topped by a platform and four footbridges, recalls the plan of the *chahar bagh*. A secret passage linked the terrace to a collection of private courtyards and buildings occupied by the harem. Among these is the palace of Jodh Bai (6), whose facade ornamented with balconies was inspired by the Rajput style. Outside the gynaeceum is the house of Birbal (7) – built in 1572, it is one of the rare buildings covered with domes. The adjacent courtyard is enclosed by three galleries, probably the stables (8). To the south-west, outside the palatine complex, stands the mosque (9).

upper part of the plateau, while below were the workshops, baths and stables, and still lower was the village of Fatehpur. By having a mosque built next to the palatine complex, Akbar affirmed the divine essence of his power.

In 1585 Akbar, who was called to fight on numerous fronts, abandoned Fatehpur for Lahore, which had a more strategic location. A lack of water has often been cited as the reason for abandoning the city, but in fact

The architecture of Fatehpur Sikri is a synthesis of Indian and Muslim arts that was desired by Akbar. Although certain ornamental figures such as the peacocks or geese belong to the Hindu iconographic repertoire, the ensemble is largely dominated by the architectural influence of Muslim Gujarat. The blocks of red sandstone are finely worked like that region's sculpture in wood – for example, the decorative elements on the interior and exterior walls of the pavilion of the Turkish sultana (opposite below). The courtyard adjacent to the house of Birbal is surrounded by three galleries probably designed to house horses and camels (opposite above). In the centre of the *diwan-i khass*, like the axis mundi, the pillar that supports the platform on which Akbar used to sit (left) evokes the decoration of the minaret of the Sidi Bachir mosque built at Ahmedabad in the 15th century.

the motive was political in nature. The city lost its population and became a ghost town, especially after the plague of 1619.

Innovations in the ritual of the court

Akbar very quickly expressed his desire to become integrated with India, rather than remain a stranger in the country. In order to improve his relations with the Hindus and, especially, the Rajputs, he stopped making the Muslims privileged citizens by abolishing discriminatory taxes on non-Muslims, such as the *jizya*. Moreover, the emperor instituted a very precise court ritual that was also intended to emphasize the centralization of power. In his fervour for unity and harmony, he adopted certain customs peculiar to Hindu ceremonial (appearances at a window, *darshan,* weighing of the prince).

The first appearance by the emperor took place early in the morning: the emperor showed himself at the balcony of a window (called *jharoka*) that dominated the walls of his palace, to greet the people, who had to prostrate themselves on seeing him. This custom enabled the population to present its petitions and to judge the ruler's state of health. Most of the emperor's morning was spent

During public audiences, or durbars, the emperor's throne was set up at the back of the reception room and raised on a kind of dais to dominate the assembly. A gilded balustrade isolated it from the members of the imperial family who were themselves separated from the dignitaries and diplomats by a silver balustrade. Behind came other dignitaries, officers and cavalrymen. A sandstone barrier separated them from the foot soldiers and servants, who were relegated to a position far from the emperor. During public audiences, the crowd had to greet the ruler by touching the ground with the right hand (*taslim*). The privileged few who could take part in private audiences had to prostrate themselves (*sidja*). Above: Akbar during a durbar.

in the public audience chamber (*diwan-i-am*) for the durbar, a public meeting during which he dealt with the current affairs of state with his ministers, generals and counsellors. Some durbars (receptions of dignitaries, commemorations, anniversaries) gave rise to great official ceremonies that were a chance to display all of the imperial pomp, and to emphasize on the same occasion the ruler's magnificence.

The afternoon and evening were devoted to the private audiences that took place in the *diwan-i khass*, where the sovereign received dignitaries and artists…. In this way, each person according to his rank could advance towards the emperor in the course of the day. In all cases, every visitor had to offer the emperor gifts whose value was proportional to his rank. In return, the emperor might

In the emperor's presence, the attendants carried standards, weapons, insignia – some decorated with yak tails – and flags covered in a red cloth (above).

also give presents, one of the most prestigious being a robe of honour that he had supposedly worn: a practice of Byzantine origin that had developed throughout the oriental world.

The court was also a place of pleasure and amusement. Although Akbar was not overfond of poetry, he did appreciate dance, song and music and, despite the protests of the doctors of Islam, he liked to relax to the sound of a melody. In a totally different category, one of Akbar's favourite entertainments was elephant fights. The emperor attached great importance to these pachyderms, which, according to him, were 'built like a mountain and endowed with the courage and ferocity of a lion'. He had established precise regulations for the upkeep of the hundreds of elephants installed in the imperial stables, and had even, according to Abul Fazl, perfected several ways of capturing these animals which in India had always symbolized strength and stability.

Like all the Mughal emperors, Akbar loved to hunt. A civil servant was responsible for organizing the royal hunts by defining a circle of several kilometres a few days before the arrival of the emperor and his guests. Men then drove animals into the heart of the circle, which was reduced in size every day. When a maximum of game was

Akbar brought musicians to his court. They were divided into seven groups so that each day had its own orchestra. Iranians, Transoxians and Kashmiris were present, but most of them came from Gwalior where the art of drupad singing flourished. One of the most renowned interpreters of this great vocal art was the singer called Tansen, a great favourite of Akbar, who brought him to the court in 1562. Above: Akbar watching female dancers. Left: a musician holding a stringed instrument.

in a minimal area, the sovereign entered the enclosure. He preferred using a bow, sword or javelin to firearms. To repel the animal, the Mughals liked to use cheetahs, a kind of Indian leopard, which they captured and trained for this purpose. They lavished attention on these predators, which were often decorated with precious collars. Hunting with falcons, highly valued in the Islamic world, was also very popular.

• In the fight at Chitor, the king with his own hand killed Jitmal, the leader of the men in the fort. He had no rival in shooting with a gun, and with the one with which he killed Jitmal, and which was called Sangram, he killed some 3000 or 4000 birds and beasts. I may be reckoned a true pupil of his. Of all sports I am most disposed to that with the gun, and in one day have shot eighteen deer. Of the austerities practised by my revered father, one was the not eating the flesh of animals. During three months of the year he ate meat, and for the remaining nine contented himself with Sufi food, and was no way pleased with the slaughter of animals. On many days and in many months this was forbidden to the people. The days and months on which he did not eat flesh are detailed in the *Akbar-nama*. •

Tuzuk-i-Jahangiri or Memoirs of Jahangir, trans. Alexander Rogers and ed. Henry Beveridge, Vol I, 1909

The Great Mughal and the arts

As capital of the empire, Fatehpur Sikri was also a centre for arts and crafts. Like Timur, the emperor considered artistic expression as a tangible testimony of his reign and of the dynasty to which he belonged. With this in mind, he had built a great number of workshops for the working of jade from Kashgar, wood and mother-of-pearl, gold and precious stones, as well as carpets. Akbar devoted himself to making haberdashery, which he considered a pleasant pastime!

The carpet workshop was run by Persian masters. The compositions were sometimes created by miniaturists, which explains the decorative aspect of certain motifs. Red backgrounds seem to have been preferred to blue ones.

Naturally, textiles occupied a predominant place in these crafts. Used daily to decorate the palaces but also the tents that shaded the court during its travels, they constituted a veritable treasure kept in the emperor's private apartments with his wardrobe. According to Abul Fazl, Akbar had a predilection for woollen clothes, so as to be like the Sufis, whose only garment was a woollen coat (*suf*). Red woollen broadcloths, called woollen broadcloths 'from Andrinople', which came from Turkey, were highly valued in this period.

Every year, a thousand costumes were made for the sovereign, and one hundred and twenty of them were laid out in protective bags, ready for his use. These clothes were stored according to the days, the months, their date of entry into the wardrobe. The same was true of the lengths of cloths that were destined to be kept as they were, or else cut up. Secretaries wrote down all the information concerning the origin of the garment on a label sewn on the bag.

The development of the imperial workshop

Like all oriental sovereigns, Akbar attached great importance to

Akbar sometimes designed his costumes. According to Abul Fazl, he liked to start fashions and made a point of imposing them on his courtiers. During his reign, men dressed in a tunic called *jama*, which fell below the knee, and was worn over trousers or *paijama*. Cloths, made of cotton or silk and in plain colours, were preferred to textiles brocaded with various motifs. The tunic was tightened at the waist by a belt of fabric, called *patka*. Fastened at the front, it had a loop which hung down at one side. The emperor developed a passion for Kashmir shawls, renowned for their lightness, and chose to wear them two at a time and dyed.

Naturally, a turban was obligatory, and removing it was a token of submission. Mughals wore turbans in the form of a 'cap', that is, flat at the top and round at the back, with a strip of fabric that passed across the centre of the skull.

Left: a courtier in typical costume. Above: a cut emerald.

books, despite the fact that he could not read. At
Fatehpur Sikri, the library (*kitab khana*) occupied
a prominent place, though the most precious
books were kept in the imperial apartments. It was
also inside this *kitab khana* that the works financed
by the sovereign were produced. A succession of
papermakers, binders, gilders,
calligraphers and painters came
there to produce the poetry
collections, biographies or tales
chosen by the emperor, who,
being illiterate, had these books
read to him. He developed a deep
respect for them. Always anxious to mark the
Mughal dynasty by his reign, he asked two masters
(Abd us-Samad and Mir Sayyid Ali),
brought back by his father from his exile
in Persia, to take control of the
imperial painting studio and to
introduce the local artists to the art

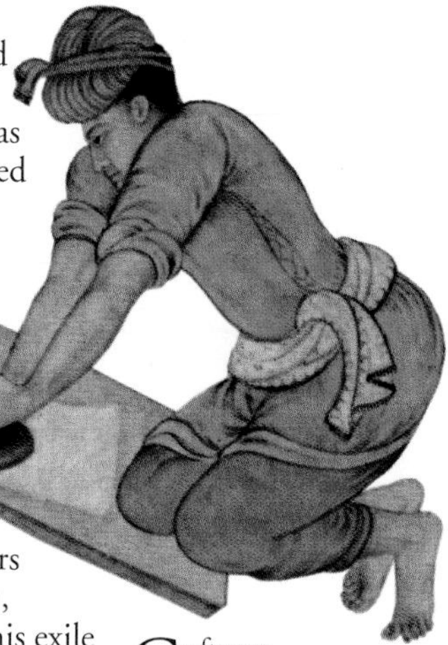

Craftsmen
of the *kitab
khana* at Fatehpur
Sikri making paper
(above and opposite).

of the miniature. These artists gradually liberated
themselves from Persian aesthetic concepts through
contact with the Hindu painters recruited at Akbar's
request, and through the observation of western works

The writing used for
transcribing the
official language,
Persian, was *nastaliq* or
cursive script.

given to the padishah by the Jesuits. These influences led to the birth of a profoundly original style. The fruit of collective work, each miniature passed through the hands of different painters, some specializing in faces, others in landscapes.... A hundred artists were thus assigned to the illustration of the *Hamza-nama*, one of the first manuscripts illustrated by the studio around 1565, which contains some 1400 paintings. The dynast's curiosity about India and its religions subsequently encouraged him to have the great Hindu epics (*Mahabharata, Ramayana, Harivamsa*) translated from Sanskrit to Persian. Around 1589 the emperor financed works of a historical nature whose purpose was to affirm the Mughals' hereditary right to govern India: this was the series of biographies (*Babur-nama, Timur-nama*), including his own, the *Akbar-nama*, written by his faithful counsellor

A painting was the work of several artists. The master of the studio began by drawing the model, on the emperor's advice. Various artists, each with his own speciality, carried on from there. Paper, introduced to India in the 14th century, was first prepared by crushing the grain with a polisher. Then the sketch was traced either in black ink or in graphite. Next, a layer of translucent white was applied to the composition, and the details drawn with red lines. Finally, the colours, made of plant- or animal-based pigments, mixed with a glue or gum arabic, were applied.

Abul Fazl. Akbar passed on to his son Jahangir this pronounced taste for painting, which remained the preferred art at the court of the Great Mughals.

From Persian painting to Mughal miniature

After the imperial Mughal studio was formed by Humayun around 1555, miniatures were organized on three vertically superimposed planes. In general, the main scene is found in the second plane, at the centre of the image, where the reader's eye falls. Under Akbar, miniatures depicting scenes of the court were rare, and instead the central figure is represented in everyday surroundings, in which nature predominates. This taste for 'animated' landscapes underlines once again an attachment to Persian aesthetic canons: closed world, abundance of vegetation (opposite, a painting of the Akbar period, from the *Hamza-nama*). However, in the 17th century, not only did the Persian influence disappear, but the emphasis was placed on the evocation of life at court. Henceforth, painting no longer merely illustrated legendary stories and tales, it served Mughal power. The depictions of sumptuous durbars prevailed. Left: a durbar of Shah Jahan. The ruler is enthroned in majesty amid his courtiers.

Art as propaganda

By permitting themselves – contrary to the principles of Islam – to depict people realistically, the Indian artists of Akbar's imperial studio created Mughal portraiture that differed from Persian and Ottoman traditions. Faces tended to be individualized by a different complexion, a moustache, a beard. Likewise, silhouettes were freed to move more effectively in their surrounding space. Under Jahangir, the influence of European images would accentuate these characteristics. He inaugurated the court portrait – realistic, seated or standing, in profile, on a plain background. Opposite: Jahangir with the great men of the world – the Sufi sheik, for whom he shows preference, the Ottoman sultan and James I of England. This type of portrait would persist in the reign of Shah Jahan (recognizable, left, by his beard). The art of this period is of uneven quality and shows a certain stiffness.

Painting in albums

Jahangir brought a fashion for *muraqqa*, albums of independent paintings which no longer illustrated a text and which were the work of a single artist. He had numerous miniatures executed, depicting flowers and animals, including those of his menagerie – a zebra from Abyssinia, a dog, all kinds of birds. This genre was to continue in the reign of Shah Jahan, notably with the miniatures from the album of Dara Shikoh (opposite, lower left), which imitated western botanical and zoological plates. In the mid-17th century more frivolous court scenes appeared, amorous encounters after nightfall (opposite top) or portraits of women with little individual identity (left). Since Mughal painters did not have access to the harem, they always depicted princesses and courtesans in an impersonal way.

In search of the truth

According to his historian Abul Fazl, as soon as his empire had been consolidated, Akbar wished to deepen his knowledge of religious matters. It seems that the padishah was not only motivated by a personal spiritual quest, but also by a desire to resolve religious conflicts that sprang from the diversity of faiths in India and interfered with the organization of his power and his unification projects.

Conscious of being God's shadow on earth, the emperor undertook in 1575 the construction in his new capital of Fatehpur Sikri of a religious house of worship that was intended for debates between the representatives of the different branches of Islam, the *Ibadat khana* or 'House of Adoration'. According to the descriptions of various witnesses from the period, this was a rectangular building, but archaeologists have not found any trace of it. During the debates, the participants formed groups according to their religious convictions, and Akbar came and went between them to discuss their arguments.

In 1577 the emperor went through a mystical crisis that led him to become a spiritual guide. Henceforth, he made a point of affirming that there was some truth in every religion, and that his role consisted in gathering them together into just one, but in such a way that they be one and all at the same time. In 1579 Akbar opened the doors of his house of worship to the Hindus, the

One Saturday the Jesuits were summoned by Akbar to the *Ibadat khana* with six mullahs (above). They presented him with a page, translated into Persian, which related the birth of Christ. A lively discussion ensued because the Jesuits said that Muhammad was not a prophet but the Antichrist.

Jains and the Parsees ... and he proclaimed that, from now on, only he could decide the state religion, thus combining spiritual and political power.

His tolerance and his openness towards other religions did not separate him from Islam, and he always declared himself to be its representative. But he was gradually to turn away from the various Muslim doctrines and draw closer to Sufism, a mystical Islamic movement which opposed any trend that tried to reduce religion to 'its legalistic and literary aspects'. In Sufism, the individual's only master is God, and ecstasy enables him to merge with the divine.

Europe at the gates of the Mughal empire

Ten years after the discovery of the passage of the Cape of Good Hope, in 1498, the Portuguese had laid the foundations of a Lusitanian empire in Asia, of which Goa, on India's south-west coast, became the centre. Throughout the 16th century they tried to expand their possessions not only in India but also in South-East Asia, in order to wrest from the Arabs the lucrative spice trade. Akbar's policy towards Portuguese expansion was clear:

Like his Timurid ancestors Akbar felt very close to the Sufi mystics, and made regular visits to Ajmer. Some Sufi orders recommend meetings during which the faithful chant litanies and invoke the name of God. A singer and musicians playing drums and flutes accompany dancing, which is sometimes a prelude to these meetings. Although complex, this dancing focuses on the body that then becomes the axis of the universe. Through this rite, the dancer seeks a lost dimension of depth and loftiness: ecstasy. 'Sufism means that God makes you die in yourself and live in him.' Below: Sufis in ecstasy.

he wanted to drive the Portuguese from India, since their maritime power on the Indian ocean thwarted Arab trade and the access of pilgrims to Islam's holy places. He even devised a plan at one time to invade Goa with the support of the sultanates of the Deccan.

Jesuits at the court of Akbar

It was in 1573, during the Gujarat military campaign, and more specifically during the siege of Surat, that Akbar for the first time came into contact with the Portuguese and especially with Christianity, the religion that was the forerunner of Islam. On several occasions he asked to meet the Jesuits so that they could answer his questions. As he found these interviews too brief, he sent in December 1578 a missive to the Jesuit college of Goa, inviting two Jesuit fathers to come to his capital of Fatehpur Sikri so that he could deepen his knowledge of what he called the Book of the Law and of the Gospel.

Seeing an opportunity to approach the Great Mughal, and secretly considering the possibility of a conversion that would bring wealth, power and glory to Portugal, the rector of the college of St Paul in Goa sent three emissaries. At dawn on 28 February 1580 Fathers Henriques and Acquaviva, followed six days later by Monserrate, entered the monumental gate of Fatehpur Sikri. Many debates were organized, carefully orchestrated by Akbar, who was always in search of truth. The Jesuit fathers, being fervent advocates of the Christian faith, and blinded

Father Monserrate, a Jesuit who stayed at the court of Akbar (below), gave a flattering portrait of the Great Mughal: 'The King is of good stature ... the configuration of his face is ordinary, and does not reflect the grandeur and dignity of the person ... being Chinese-like as the Mughals usually are.' Later, the cleric added: 'His eyes are small but extremely vivid and when he looks at you it seems as if they hurt you with their brightness, and thus nothing escapes his notice ... and they also reveal sharpness of mind and keenness of intellect.'

by the desire to convert the sovereign, had no consideration for the spirit of universality that motivated Akbar. In that sense, their mission, which ended in 1582, was a failure. Later, other Christian embassies, especially Jesuits, came to the emperor's court with no greater success.

For his succession, the superstitious Akbar relied on chance by having two elephants fight (below): one belonged to Salim, the other to Khusrau. Prince Salim's was victorious, which left a bitter taste in the old man's mouth. The empire was then prey to numerous rebellions, and Akbar was conscious of his successor's lack of ability (left, Salim, the future Jahangir, contemplating his father's portrait). On the very evening of this decisive battle, 20 September 1605, Akbar became seriously ill.

The young prince Salim rebels and claims the throne

When old and tired, Akbar had to confront the ambitions of his son Salim. While he was waging war in the Deccan, Akbar was forced to rush back to Agra on learning that his son and heir had just had himself proclaimed padishah at Allahabad. In a spirit of openness and dialogue, he dispatched his faithful Abul Fazl to Salim. Having always mistrusted his father's favourite minister, the prince organized an ambush in which the counsellor was killed. On hearing this news, Akbar, who was overwhelmed with grief, cursed his son and planned to name Khusrau, his grandson and Salim's eldest son, as his successor. However, falling prey to an attack of dysentery, the first Great Mughal died on 27 October 1605, leaving, after a reign of fifty years, an empire that was as glorious as the Safavid dynasty in Persia or the Ottoman empire in Turkey.

In the 17th century the Mughal empire reached its peak. Although its frontiers were regularly pushed back, its wealth and splendour made it one of the most dazzling courts in the oriental world. Akbar's successors, too confident in the stability of the structures of state that he had set in place, did not always perceive the need for reforms, and their power declined.

CHAPTER 3

AN OPULENT EMPIRE: JAHANGIR AND SHAH JAHAN

Having been consecrated padishah, Prince Salim took the name of Jahangir, 'World Seizer' because 'the duty of a sovereign is to govern the world'. In this miniature (opposite), the majestic emperor, accompanied by a lion, walks the path traced by Akbar. Right: the Great Mughal Shah Jahan.

It was a mature man of thirty-seven who, in October 1605, succeeded a father whose glory still resounded in the four corners of India. Unlike his ancestors, Jahangir was no conqueror, and preferred to enjoy the comfort that life at court brought him. His attachment to protocol and the heavy organization of his days very quickly prevented him from taking an active part in the command of his armies – especially as his liking for alcohol, which had already killed his brothers, often left him apathetic. Paradoxically, the emperor was feared for his rages and his terrible acts of revenge. The Europeans who stayed at the court were struck by the cruelty of the punishments he inflicted on his enemies, which ranged from blinding to poisoning.

Khusrau's revolt

Jahangir had inherited a stable empire, and the first fifteen years of his reign were relatively peaceful. The only shadow cast on this picture was the rebellion by his son Khusrau. Ever since ascending the throne, Jahangir had been opposed by a faction led by the Rajput Man Singh, who favoured Khusrau, his son-in-law. In order to nip this opposition in the bud, Jahangir named Man Singh governor of the far-off province of Bengal, and brought Khusrau to his side at court. However, a few months later, Khusrau revolted at Lahore, compelling Jahangir to gather his armies and march towards the northern provinces. Conquered, Khusrau was imprisoned and his followers cruelly punished. Among them was the Sikh guru Arjun, whose execution stirred up the anger of the Sikhs towards Mughal power. To smother all

Jahangir's enthronement took place at Agra (opposite) in the presence of a mixed crowd that had come from India and the Orient. The new sovereign wanted to be an impartial dispenser of justice. From the very start of his reign, in order to make good any injustice that might be committed against one of his subjects, he decided to have a golden chain, furnished with sixty bells, strung up between Agra's Red Fort and the nearby River Yamuna. Any victim could, by shaking this chain, attract attention to his case. Jahangir was very strong, and devoted himself to hunting and combat sports. Lion hunting was the emperor's privilege (below, Jahangir killing a lion).

ambitions by the Rajputs, and urged on by his third son Khurram, he quietly subjugated their chief, Amar Singh of Mewar. Similarly, he subdued once and for all any Afghan ambitions in Bengal. There the incompetence of successive governors had revived the hopes of his hereditary enemies, who were always ready to seize power.

During military campaigns, the Great Mughal had vast cloth encampments set up, protected by an enclosure. The tents were white, apart from the emperor's quarters, which were red. Below: Khurram receives the submission of the rana of Mewar.

Jahangir took a timid approach in the Deccan, although, like his father, he wanted to invade the south of the subcontinent. The imperial troops were led by his two sons Parviz and Khurram. With great difficulty, they defeated the sultan Malik Ambar, who lost his

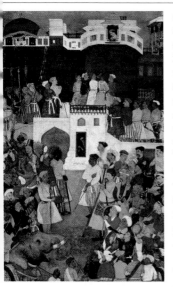

capital Ahmednagar. To thank Khurram, Jahangir offered him the title of Shah Jahan, 'Emperor of the World'. Despite this successful incursion into the Deccan, the Mughal armies could not subjugate the powerful kingdoms of Golconda and Bijapur. They were supported by the Persians, who were very much present in these states. The Mughals did not, however, relent, and continued to harass the Deccan sultanates. In 1616 Khurram was named commander in chief in the Deccan, in place of Parviz.

Jahangir kept the custom of the *jharoka*. At either side of the imperial window in the Agra fort (left) he had installed a sculptured wooden elephant, plated with silver.

The reign of Shah Abbas I (below) marked the pinnacle of the Safavid dynasty which had taken power in Persia in 1502. In 1598 he moved his capital to Ispahan, in the centre of the country. A great patron of the arts, passionate about architecture, he made it a city renowned for its refined pavilions, built in the middle of gardens.

Mughal India and Persia

Despite Persian interference in the affairs of the Deccan, Jahangir was satisfied with the good relations that had been established with Shah Abbas I. Mughal India had never been on such good terms with its Persian enemy. Embassies, vying with each other to exchange rich presents and and fine words, crossed between Ispahan and Agra. But the shah was laying claim to the frontier city of Kandahar, then in a Mughal protectorate. Being more calculating than Jahangir, he took advantage of the exceptional trust that had become established between the two countries, and the weak level of defence of the fortress, and seized it in 1622. Taken by surprise, Jahangir tried to set up a last-minute alliance with the Uzbeks, but they showed little enthusiasm. He then sought the help of his son Khurram, who refused to travel far from the centre of India, fearing that his brothers might seize the power that was unravelling in Jahangir's hands. Kandahar slipped from the clutches of the Mughals.

The 'reign' of Nur Jahan

In 1611 the emperor fell madly in love with a
Persian woman called Mihr un-Nisa – in fact he
had loved her ever since childhood. Married to a
dignitary, she had left Agra to follow her husband
to a post in Bengal. After the unexplained death
of this embarrassing husband, she returned to the
heart of the imperial court, and married Jahangir
a few months later. Henceforth, she who was
called Nur Mahal, 'Light of the Palace',
before becoming Nur Jahan, 'Light of the
World', surrounded herself with a clan
comprising, among others, her father,
Itimad ud-Daula, a Persian adventurer
who had become Jahangir's prime
minister, and her brother Asaf
Khan. In a way, by imposing
these Persians on the court,
she strengthened the Muslim
orthodoxy that Jahangir, who
wanted to avoid all religious
conflict, did not try to
oppose. Son of a Rajput
princess, he knew and
respected the principles of
Hinduism, and, even if he
sometimes ordered the destruction
of temples, he acted more out of
a wish to impose his authority on
potential Hindu rebels than out
of religious sectarianism.
Moreover, he was interested
in Christianity, and looked
favourably on the Jesuits who
visited the court regularly. Tempted at
one time by a conversion to Catholicism, he seems
to have decided against it in order to avoid any pressure
from Portuguese power.

Secluded behind the perforated windows of the harem,
Nur Jahan defended Islam and firmly held the reins of
power. Everybody agreed that she was beautiful and

Islam allows a man to
marry four women on
the condition that he
treats them in the same
way. However, in taking
Mihr un-Nisa as his
second wife, Jahangir
promoted her to the
rank for first wife.
Henceforth, she asked
that the women of the
harem should call her
Nur Mahal (above,
the empress with
her attendants).

intelligent. Weakened by illness and alcoholism, Jahangir relied on the decisions of this wife who directed the empire with competence, and whose portrait decorated the reverse of the silver coinage minted by the emperor.

A skilfully orchestrated succession

From 1622 the enfeebled emperor preferred the temperate climate of Kashmir to the court with its intrigues. Nur Jahan, who was then at the pinnacle of her power, sensed that the dynast's end was approaching, and tried to safeguard her future by supporting Jahangir's youngest son, Shahryar, to whom she gave her daughter in marriage. A fervent Sunni, Shahryar was supported by orthodox Muslims, who were critical of the rather open political attitudes of Khusrau, the designated heir kept in prison by his father. This was reckoning without the other brothers, Parviz and Khurram. Nur Jahan made a temporary alliance with the latter, and tightened their links by presenting him with his future wife, Arjumand Banu, who was her niece, the daughter of Asaf Khan. The mysterious and opportune deaths of Khusrau in 1622 and of Parviz in 1626 seem to have been orchestrated by Khurram, whose ambition knew no bounds.

Rubies, diamonds, emeralds and pearls were the stones most prized by the Mughals, who were great lovers of jewels. Above: an 18th-century Mughal necklace.

A single approach, guarded by eunuchs, led to the harem located at the back of the citadel, not far from the imperial apartments. The numerous women of the Mughal court owed obedience to the first wife. They were secluded and often idle, spending most of their time scheming, in their anxiety to please the king, and putting on perfume and finery. They often transferred their affection to other women in the harem (following pages).

Whereas silk often came from China and was fashioned in the imperial workshops of Agra or Lahore, cotton was largely produced in India. The finest muslins, which enhanced the beauty of Jahangir's tunics, were produced in Bengal. Sometimes the cloth was embroidered or painted with floral motifs like this hunting jacket from the reign of Jahangir (below). To complete his outfits, the emperor abandoned the 'caplike' turban established by Akbar and instead wore a round turban, decorated with precious stones and egret feathers.

A sophisticated court

Although Jahangir was not a great reformer concerned about the interests of his empire, he was nevertheless an enlightened sovereign, well read and an aesthete, who decided to make the imperial court a centre of refinement. Through his splendour the emperor tried to impress foreign ambassadors and local populations in order to command the respect owed to his rank.

Unlike other Mughal dynasts, he did not have a new capital built; he imposed Agra and Lahore as imperial cities even though, in the face of the threats that hung over the empire, he moved this centre to Kabul, Ajmer or Mandu, building immense cloth camps to which the court was transferred. Artists and craftsmen followed the emperor wherever he went. Jahangir attached great importance to the decorative arts. Every object used in his daily life had to be a work of art, like his daggers to which he devoted long passages in his memoirs, the *Tuzuk-i-Jahangiri*. He seems to have taken a great deal of interest in clothes. Judging by the numerous miniatures produced during his reign, he was an innovator by having garments cut from the finest silk and cotton fabrics.

A great connoisseur of Persian poetry, he was also curious about nature. He loved to observe landscapes, flowers, animals and even went as far as dissecting a bird to understand its characteristics.

Kashmir, a 'paradise on earth'

Jahangir was very fond of Kashmir, far from the crushing heat of the Delhi plain, where the pure air and nature brought him a feeling of well-being and serenity. His prolonged stays in this province led him to have gardens built around Lake Dal. In 1619 at Srinagar he undertook the construction of the most marvellous of these, the Shalimar, 'Abode of Love', against a mountain. The central water course, the garden's spinal column, crossed three terraces in a labyrinth of sophisticated fountains. Each platform was ornamented with a *chahar bagh*, where fruit trees and beds of flowers constituted a veritable hymn to nature. Whereas the first terrace, giving on to the lake, was public, the second was reserved for the emperor and the third, protected from view by rows of plane trees, was intended for the harem. Anxious to emulate their sovereign, his courtiers and ministers also had magnificent gardens built, whose luxuriance of vegetation and fountains tried to imitate the Paradise that was promised to every good Muslim.

Funerary art under Jahangir

Jahangir was not very interested in architecture (apart from the construction of Jahangirabad, present-day

The throne, or *aurang*, symbol of imperial power, was generally made of wood, sometimes encrusted with precious stones or plated with gold or silver leaf (opposite above).

Jahangir designed the shapes of his daggers himself, and submitted his plans to his relations and courtiers for comment.

Dacca, in Bengal), but nevertheless he attached some importance to having the mausoleums of his father, Akbar, and his father-in-law, Itimad ud-Daula, built near Agra. The architecture of Akbar's tomb, at Sikandra, emphasized the personality of the deceased sovereign, who always wanted to free himself from received ideas. In having Humayun's mausoleum built, Akbar had displayed, on the one hand, a taste for novelty while still paying homage to his Timurid ancestors and,

Akbar's mausoleum (below) rises in five storeys; a terrace topped by three storeys of *chhatri* in red sandstone, which evoke the *panch mahal* of Fatehpur Sikri. At the top of this open-work pyramid, the emperor's cenotaph stands in the centre of a quadrangular platform of white marble, paved like a checkerboard and enclosed by a gallery with perforated stone screens, or *jali*. Above left: the mausoleum's entrance gate.

on the other hand, his originality by designing the plans of his own tomb himself. His coffin was destined to lie in a small chamber on the third floor, the walls of which are supposed to have been painted with Christian scenes depicting, amongst others, the Virgin Mary. Precious objects, carpets and fabrics were also set out in this room, but the whole thing was pillaged and damaged in the 17th century. This mausoleum was the last to be built in red sandstone, which was soon replaced with white marble.

Built in 1626 in the middle of a *chahar bagh* garden, the mausoleum of Nur Jahan's father, Itimad ud-Daula, is an edifice of modest proportions, consisting entirely of white marble encrusted with semi-precious stones, which foreshadows the architecture of Shah Jahan's reign.

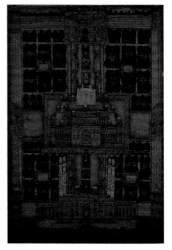

Above: plan of Akbar's mausoleum at Sikandra.

Built on the orders of Nur Jahan, the mausoleum of Jahangir's minister (left and plan above) lies on a terrace in the middle of a garden along the river, near Agra. Since Itimad-ud Daula was not royal, its proportions remained modest: five rooms arranged in a quincunx with a rectangular chamber at each side. On the second floor, a pavilion with *jali* protects the cenotaph (page 86, an interior view). With its sophisticated decoration, it is reminiscent of the civil architecture of the palaces rather than of that of the tombs. Red sandstone is replaced with white marble delicately inlaid with foliated scrolls and flowers in semi-precious stones. The Persian decorative themes, cypresses or wine bottles, underline the origin of Nur Jahan's father. The four octagonal turrets of the mausoleum (cross-section page 86) were transformed into four minarets at Jahangir's tomb in Lahore (top left) and at the Taj Mahal (top centre).

Jahangir's succession

When Shah Jahan was born in 1592, his grandfather Akbar, who had conquered the whole of North India, was so happy about the birth of this third grandson that he gave him the name of Khurram, meaning 'Joy'. The

In order to ensure that the stars would act favourably towards his son's bad health, Jahangir established a weighing ceremony for Khurram's sixteenth lunar birthday (left). Previously, princes were only weighed once a year, at the time of their solar birthday. This Hindu custom, adopted by Akbar, consisted of weighing the emperor and princes, and distributing to the poor (then, subsequently, to the women of the harem) their weight in rare commodities. There were twelve commodities: gold, silver, silk, perfume, copper, iron, butter, starch, salt, and different kinds of grain. Below: portrait of Shah Jahan on horseback.

conjunction of the stars was identical to that at the birth of Timur, and predicted a brilliant future for the young prince. Khurram was very close not only to his illustrious grandfather, but also to his father, whom he nevertheless reproached for his being partial to wine. Having seen his uncle die from the ravages caused by alcohol, he harboured a great aversion to drink. Jahangir's right-hand man and designated successor, Khurram entered into conflict with the emperor in 1623. This disagreement was hatched in part by Nur Jahan, who wanted to protect her interests and obtain the support of the ulemas (scholars), guarantors of the Muslim state, and who put forward the vulnerable Shahryar. Jahangir, weakened and under the influence of his wife, relied on the latter's wishes.

In autumn 1627, while Jahangir was dying, the different factions began to oppose each other to support the future emperor. Khurram, confined to the Deccan on Jahangir's orders, moved towards the capital. In November, when his father's death was announced, the impatient Shahryar had himself proclaimed emperor and seized the treasury of Lahore. Khurram, supported by the army, was sure of victory. He asked his faithful father-in-law, Asaf Khan, to defeat Shahryar, and then to eliminate all the pretenders to the throne. This cruel attitude underlined Shah Jahan's decisive mind, which characterized him throughout his reign. Disowned by her brother and nephew, Nur Jahan accepted her defeat with dignity. As soon as he had been consecrated emperor, Shah Jahan exiled her to Lahore, where she

While he was still only a prince, Shah Jahan was invited by Nur Jahan to come to the Mina Bazar, a festival established by Akbar that allowed the palace women to sell fabrics and jewels every month. It was on this occasion that he fell for a young girl of fourteen, Arjumand Banu, the daughter of Asaf Khan. Jahangir arranged the marriage, which only took place five years later. The girl (above), henceforth called Mumtaz Mahal, 'Chosen One of the Palace', had a pleasant and unassuming manner. She followed her husband into forced exile in the Deccan and gave him fourteen children. Most portraits depicting Mumtaz Mahal date from the 19th century (above).

devoted her time to having Jahangir's tomb embellished. After the splendid festivities given in his honour, Shah Jahan began his reign by taking a firm stand. After the lack of political audacity of Jahangir, who, through his sumptuous spending and his free-and-easy attitude, had placed finances and administration in a woeful state, the empire needed to be consolidated and the padishah's authority restored. While not a great reformer, Shah Jahan buckled down to this task of consolidation.

Shah Jahan, a strong ruler, reaffirms Mughal power

All attempts at opposition by the Rajputs were quickly subdued. Moreover, despite being a Sunni, the emperor decided to dismiss excessively strict Muslim dignitaries. In 1632, confronted by the discontent of certain orthodox individuals, he found himself compelled to order the destruction of Hindu temples, especially at Benares, in order to ensure their support once more. Shortly afterwards, he started a campaign to demolish cult sites, which were replaced with mosques, and he forced Hindus to renounce religious practices that were judged to be 'disturbing' for Muslims, like cremation near cemeteries.

This was the beginning of discriminatory policies: henceforth the Hindus had to wear tunics that buttoned on the left, while Muslims did theirs up on the right. At the same time, he abolished certain reforms brought in by Akbar, such as the divine era (*ilahi*) and prostration in front of the throne.

More or less in the same period, he took an interest in the Portuguese community of Hugli, in Bengal, a province far from the central power which had let the Portuguese organize themselves there. The latter lost no time in fortifying their possessions, and in levying taxes. During organized raids on neighbouring villages, they compelled the population to convert to Christianity, and did not hesitate to carry off youngsters to sell them. The emperor decided to quell the pretensions of the Portuguese, who did not try to support him during his revolt against his father, and he sacked Hugli. Subsequently, he would remain suspicious of the Portuguese, and of Europeans in general, and regularly led campaigns to limit their ambitions.

Shah Jahan, in his turn, wishes to subjugate the Deccan

Having waged war for a long time in the Deccan, Shah Jahan wanted to re-establish the policy begun by Akbar and Jahangir in southern India, that is, the imposition of Mughal suzerainty on the independent Muslim kingdoms. It was not a question of conquering Golconda and Bijapur by force, but of subduing

Shah Jahan (below) did not only want portraits in profile. Probably influenced by European painting, the emperor asked his painters to give him a halo. His idealized face is always depicted with the beard of orthodox Muslims which his predecessors refused to have.

Under Shah Jahan the Mughal army continued to be very powerful. It protected the state against invasions and revolts and helped to extend the empire.

them so they would bring their annual tribute to the Mughal treasury. From the beginning of his reign, Shah Jahan was confronted by the insurrection of Khan Jahan Lodi, who had been appointed viceroy of the Deccan by Jahangir, and who was rapidly subdued by the imperial armies. Thanks to the complicity of the son of Malik Ambar, chief of the sultan's armies, Shah Jahan's armies subjugated the state of Ahmednagar, which had previously escaped Jahangir. In 1635 the sultanate of Golconda, which was in no position to resist, surrendered in its turn.

Conversely, the sultan of Bijapur, who in 1631 had succeeded in making Asaf Khan retreat, was still opposed to the padishah. In order to prevent the Mughal armies entering his capital, he ordered its approaches to be flooded. This was a waste of effort, because the enemy troops ravaged the neighbouring countryside. In 1636 the emperor sent his son, Aurangzeb, and, confronted by the forces deployed by the Great Mughal, the sultan of Bijapur found himself compelled to pay allegiance and to sign a treaty of vassalage. Aurangzeb was then appointed viceroy of the Deccan for the second time. Being more radical than his father, he tried to subjugate the two recalcitrant kingdoms by force. However, they were given some respite, thanks to the intervention of Shah Jahan, who only wished to impose a profitable vassalage on them.

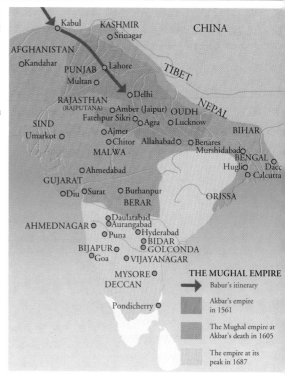

THE MUGHAL EMPIRE

→ Babur's itinerary

Akbar's empire in 1561

The Mughal empire at Akbar's death in 1605

The empire at its peak in 1687

In its initial stages, Babur's empire was limited to the plain of the Ganges. Akbar conquered the whole of the northern Indian provinces and reduced part of the Deccan to vassalage. His successors tried to maintain the empire, which expanded under Aurangzeb with the submission of the Deccan from 1686 to 1687. After taking possession of the eastern states, the British settled in central-west India, in the Punjab and Sind.

Shah Jahan also seeks to conquer Samarkand

Once the Deccan was subdued, the sovereign's interest turned to the cradle of his ancestors: Central Asia and its city of enlightenment, Samarkand. Being a fervent admirer of his ancestor Timur, Shah Jahan longed to make the Timurid capital a Mughal imperial city. In 1646, taking advantage of the Uzbeks' internal quarrels, he took the opportunity to march on Samarkand by attacking Balkh. The attack was led by his son Murad Bakhsh, who was not very aggressive, and who also detested these arid and mountainous lands, so when he was halfway there he asked his father if he could return home.

It was Aurangzeb, the conqueror of the family, who took his place. Faced with the Mughal prince's determination, the Uzbeks, who were no match for their opponents, sought the support of the Persian armies. However, they did not appreciate the Mughal advances. The Mughals suffered a crushing defeat. Samarkand was certainly not destined to become a Mughal possession. Just like Babur, Shah Jahan would never abandon hope of conquering the 'blue pearl of the Orient'.

Whereas Samarkand was a dream, Kandahar was a reality. Once again, after the Persian governor had been bought, the city passed into Mughal control. In 1649 the Persians retook the fortress. The emperor did not give in, and started several campaigns, the most disastrous of which was led by Dara Shikoh, Shah Jahan's designated heir. Dara, poet, intellectual, and troubled prince, was a pitiful soldier.

Shah Jahan had his life written by several historians. This painting (below), taken from the *Padshah-nama*, a biography written by Abdul Hamid Lahori, depicts the handing over of the keys of a newly conquered city to one of Shah Jahan's generals. It is probably Kandahar, the symbol of the eternal quarrel between Mughals and Persians.

Shah Jahan the builder, or the triumph of white marble

During his reign, Shah Jahan expanded and consolidated the empire built by his ancestors. Anxious to leave his mark, he began an important building campaign. Immediately after his accession, he modified the architectural structure both of the fort of Lahore, Jahangir's main capital and a favourite spot during the early part of his reign, and of the Red Fort of Agra, where he rapidly set up his court. Light pavilions of white marble rose in the middle of flower gardens, replacing once and for all the red sandstone architecture built under Akbar.

Wishing to live in the capital of his ancestor Humayun, Shah Jahan undertook the creation of his own city, Shahjahanabad (now Old Delhi), at Delhi. The first stone was laid in 1639, and in 1648 the city was completed – its renown reached the borders of the Muslim world. From now on an imperial residence, the Red Fort of Delhi, or Lal Qila, had a symmetrical plan comprising a collection of buildings with fine arcades. A water course crossed gardens and buildings, bringing the coolness and babbling that were indispensable to the well-being of every oriental prince. Although sober, its architectural decor was primarily floral. Shah Jahan took

Since he suffered in the heat, Shah Jahan demolished the buildings of Agra's Red Fort from the reign of Akbar and built hypostyles that allowed the air to circulate. Above: the *diwan-i khass* at Agra (right), and detail of a white marble column inlaid with stone flowers. Below: the royal apartments in the Red Fort of Agra benefited from having the cool river nearby.

up the flowering plant motif that was inspired by the European herbariums of the 16th century and perfected by his father's artists. Pillars, colonnades, thrones, and bas-reliefs were from now on decorated with these flowers made of hard stones inlaid with white marble.

As a Muslim, Shah Jahan also had several mosques built, including the 'Pearl Mosque', Moti Masjid, in the Red Fort at Agra. However, the indisputable masterpiece, the symbol of his faith, was certainly the Jami Masjid of Delhi. In 1650, beyond the thick sandstone ramparts of Lal Qila, the sovereign ordered the construction of one of the subcontinent's biggest mosques. Slightly raised, so that it dominated the city, it was inspired by the great mosque constructed by Akbar at Fatehpur Sikri.

Whereas he had the great mosque of Delhi built outside Lal Qila, Shah Jahan felt the need to build a mosque inside the Red Fort itself when he settled at Agra. The Moti Masjid in white marble (above) has a large courtyard and seven archways.

'Regulations for house-building in general are necessary. They are required for the comfort of the army and are a source of splendour for the government.'
Abul Fazl
Ain-i-Akbari, trans. Heinrich Blochmann, 1873

Breaking with the nomadic custom of living in tents, the Mughals built vast residences in the heart of their capitals. After Akbar, who created Fatehpur Sikri, Shah Jahan settled in Delhi, where he built his own city, Shahjahanabad. Mughal power was now well established, and its stability had to be expressed in an orderly architecture. The plan of the Red Fort is divided into two symmetrical zones arranged at either side of a central axis: to the west, the bazaar and administration; to the north, the gardens and residences of the nobles; to the east, the emperor's apartments; and, to the south, the harem (left, a drawing from the late 18th century).

Symbol of Mughal splendour: the Taj Mahal

Following some disturbances in the Deccan, Shah Jahan and Mumtaz Mahal settled at Burhanpur. On 7 June 1631 the emperor was overwhelmed with grief and put on his white mourning garment: Mumtaz had just died while giving birth to their fourteenth child. From then on, Shah Jahan had only two preoccupations: the administration of his empire, and, in order to pay homage to his wife, the construction of a mausoleum whose beauty would symbolize the greatness of his love. Shah Jahan chose the site of Agra, on the banks of the Yamuna, to build the 'Tomb of Light' (*rauza-i munavvara*), better known by the name of Taj Mahal, a corruption of Mumtaz Mahal. Work began in 1632 and the building's fabric was finished eight years later. It seems that the emperor himself made a major contribution to the conception of the building, but there are no specific details. However, the speed and perfection of the building's execution suggest that its plans and principal ideas were drawn up well before the monument was built.

• Only let this one teardrop, the Taj Mahal, glisten spotlessly bright on the cheek of time for ever and ever. O King! You sought to charm time with the magic of beauty and weave a garland that would bind formless death with deathless form!…

Inspired by the tomb of Humayun at Delhi, the Taj Mahal revived the Timurid tradition of great edifices topped with a dome, a concept that had been abandoned during Jahangir's reign. However, in contrast to Humayun's tomb, which stood at the intersection of two water courses, in the centre of a *chahar bagh*, the Taj Mahal stands at the end of the garden, enclosed by a wall with four gates, three of which are false.

The monumental gate is built of red sandstone and opens opposite the mausoleum of white marble which is reflected in the central water course. Built on a terrace overlooking the Yamuna, it looks down on the garden, a vision of Paradise. The four minarets that frame it complete the ensemble, which soars towards the sky. Lower down, at either side, are the two red sandstone buildings, a mosque and a guest house, which sanctify the place. Originally, beds planted with flowers of various kinds and with fruit trees contributed to the image of Paradise as evoked by the Koran.

The mausoleum stands still and unmoving in its place. Here on the dusty earth, it keeps death tenderly covered in the shroud of memory.[9]

Rabindranath Tagore,
Indian Bengali poet
(1861–1941)

Below: view of the Taj Mahal.

The construction of the Taj Mahal used thousands of workers, who laboured under the orders of several architects, the best known of which was Ustad Ahmad Lahori. Entirely built of white marble from the quarries of Makrana (Rajasthan), the edifice has a square plan with five rooms laid out in a quincunx. The principal room (left), below which is the crypt containing the tombs of Mumtaz Muhal and Shah Jahan, is octagonal in shape, evoking the eight gardens of Paradise. The two cenotaphs are surrounded by a delicately perforated marble grille, inlaid with floral motifs. The bulbous dome that covers the central chamber is also surrounded by four *chhatri*. The allusion to Paradise, already perceptible in the very conception of the Taj Mahal, is stressed by the tracery of foliated scrolls and flowers in semi-precious stones that adorns the mausoleum's walls. Opposite top: the southern entrance. Opposite below: the Taj Mahal and its water gardens.

The marvels of Mughal art

By choosing to live in the closed world of the court, Jahangir invigorated the artists of the imperial studios. Although dominated by architecture, Shah Jahan's reign was nonetheless an auspicious period for all the decorative arts. One of the symbols of the splendour of the Great Mughal's court is unquestionably the famous Peacock Throne, entirely made of gold encrusted with precious stones. On his enthronement,

Because Islam does not recommend the depiction of living beings, the floral motif has always inspired Muslim artists. With Shah Jahan, it reached its peak and became the archetype of Mughal decorative art (above, an enamelled box). Constantly present, it also decorates carpets and textiles (left, a hanging, probably embroidered at Ahmedabad).

Shah Jahan's taste for floral decorations in semi-precious stones inlaid in white marble (opposite, detail of a piece from the Taj Mahal) seem to have been influenced by Italy.

Shah Jahan drew gold and precious stones from the royal treasury to have a throne made whose magnificence was to be without equal. Seven years later, the emperor took his seat on this new pedestal.

Very well-read, and himself a calligrapher, Shah Jahan favoured the art of the book. Although Persian expression had pride of place, the emperor had a very high regard for Indian literature, and had numerous vernacular works adapted from Hindi or Sanskrit into Persian. Like his ancestors, he had a historian by the name of Abdul Hamid Lahori write the chronicles of his reign under the title of *Padsha-nama*. At the same time, album painting reached its peak with magnificent portraits. Like his father, the emperor loved to have himself depicted in the midst of his court. His portraits show great refinement, but a slight idealization of features. The courtiers were also depicted. Their silhouettes, often represented in profile, stand out against a sea-green background borrowed from the paintings of the Deccan, a region that was partly a Mughal protectorate. In addition to these depictions of nobles and generals, special homage was paid to holy men, dervishes or yogis.

Shah Jahan collected jades, and also appreciated other hard stones. He asked his artists to abandon the austerity of the pieces commissioned by his ancestors, and to take inspiration from the floral motif that is so characteristic of his reign (above, a nephrite cup and, left, a decorative piece for a turban).

An empire coveted by four sovereigns

After a reign of thirty years, Shah Jahan became seriously ill in 1657. On learning this, the Mughal's four sons laid claim to the title of emperor.

The eldest, Dara Shikoh, trained in affairs of state, was considered the future padishah. Aged forty-three, he was governor of the Punjab, where he was well liked. Highly cultured and well versed in Hinduism, he took up his pen to try and compare the Hindu doctrine of the bhakti (devotion to God leading to nirvana) with Sufism, the mystical branch of Islam.

He himself was a fervent Sufi, and belonged to a particularly tolerant sect of qadirs; this was not to the liking of the ulemas, who feared the enthronement of a prince who would not give priority to the rules of Islam. His difficult personality – he could not take criticism – and the fact that he spoke a different language from the ulemas alienated part of the court.

Compared to such a personality, his brothers Shah Shuja and Murad Bakhsh cut sorry figures. The rather affable Shah Shuja governed Bengal. Unlike his elder brother, he had embraced Shiite Islam, though without renouncing luxury or the pleasures of life. As for Murad Bakhsh, he was an excellent soldier who held one of India's key provinces, Gujarat, but his dissolute ways caused doubts about his ability to govern.

The most discreet but also most ambitious of the four brothers was undoubtedly Aurangzeb, 'Ornament of the Throne'. Constantly occupied with military campaigns, he was not used to the court and harboured a certain

Dara Shikoh had a pleasing appearance, and loved women (above, the prince in his harem). He was also a great intellectual who undertook to bring together the theological ideas of Sufism and Hinduism. Among other things, he translated into Persian the Sanskrit text of the *Upanishads*.

Opposite: the Red Fort at Agra, the emperor's last abode, and the Taj Mahal.

In the 17th century a French traveller and jeweller, Jean-Baptiste Tavernier, described the end of Shah Jahan's life: 'In his old age he committed an indiscretion; and, moreover, used some drugs of so stringent a character that they brought on a malady which nearly brought him to the grave. This necessitated his shutting himself up for two or three months in his harem with his women, and during that time he showed himself to his people but rarely, and at long intervals; this caused them to believe that he was dead. For custom requires these Kings to show themselves in public three times every week, or, at the very least, every fifteen days.' (*Travels in India*, trans. V. Ball, Vol. I, 1889.)

contempt for the princes and courtiers who were far too preoccupied with intrigues and pleasures. As a child, he was engrossed in reading Muslim texts. As an adult, he ferociously defended Sunni Islam, and the clerics saw in him a true soldier of the Islamic faith. Although Indian blood flowed in his veins, he had a certain admiration for his ancestors from Central Asia. Stamped with a kind of idealism, he longed to expand the Mughal empire, in part to comply with the Timurid ideal, in part to impose Islamic order.

While Aurangzeb's religious politics were inciting the non-Muslim populations to rebel, the European presence in India continued to grow. In the 18th century the British and the French confronted each other, and the British eventually became the masters of India. In 1858, after the Sepoy Rebellion, they sent the last Mughal ruler into exile.

CHAPTER 4

THE DECLINE OF A DYNASTY

Heir to the splendour of the Mughal empire, Bahadur Shah II (opposite) was a mere plaything in the hands of the British, who used the old sovereign to legitimize their power. British domination nevertheless brought a certain stability to India, which had been torn apart in the 18th century by strife between the different ethnic and religious communities.

Aurangzeb was a great strategist, and rapidly seized Agra. In June 1658 he had his father imprisoned in the Red Fort where he was to stay until his death, eight years later. The terrified Shah Shuja withdrew to Burma (now Myanmar) where he asked for asylum from Magh Raja, who refused to help him. Pursued by a follower of Aurangzeb, Shah Shuja disappeared in the jungle. As for Murad Bakhsh, he claimed the title of emperor, and as

On 29 May 1658, on the plain of Samugarh, near Agra, Aurangzeb confronted the 50,000 soldiers led by Dara Shikoh (below): a poorly prepared army that lacked coordination in the face of the perfect

such accepted an invitation from Aurangzeb who got him drunk, imprisoned him, and then had him executed in 1661.

However, his most formidable enemy remained Dara Shikoh. Fleeing across North India, he decided not to head for Kabul, and instead went to Sind, from where he secretly hoped to reach Persia. His journey was ended because of the treason of a Pathan prince. Dara Shikoh and his son were taken prisoner and sent to Aurangzeb. Having been dragged through the streets of Delhi, Dara was condemned to death by the doctors of Islam for heresy. He was decapitated in 1659 by a slave that he had

organization of Aurangzeb's troops. In the course of the battle, Dara Shikoh had to leave his wounded elephant and take a horse. On seeing the abandoned pachyderm, his followers believed he was dead, and fled. In the subsequent confusion, Dara tried to reach Agra. He was taken prisoner shortly afterwards.

once mistreated, and his body was thrown near the tomb of his ancestor Humayun. His son Suleiman was also imprisoned, and died a few years later from the effects of the drug that was administered to him every day. Aurangzeb's reign could now start in earnest.

The first years that he was in power were marked by a certain continuity: in parallel with the policy of conquest, which enabled him to push back the empire's frontiers (towards Assam and Bengal), he tried to maintain the path of 'harmonious cohabitation' between the multiple components of the empire, as his predecessors had done. However, from 1660 revolts sprang up, upsetting this delicate balance. It was finally shattered by Aurangzeb's revival of Muslim orthodoxy as a means to combat the non-Muslim population.

The rise of opposition

Although the Rajputs had collaborated with Mughal power since the time of Akbar, some of them nonetheless remained active opponents. In wishing to annex the province of Marwar, Aurangzeb aroused old antagonisms. In 1678, on the death of Rajah Jaswant Singh Rathor, who was bereft of an heir, the Great Mughal decided to impose one of his own men as the head of the kingdom, and hence to join this province to the empire. This problem of succession provoked a large Rajput uprising. The bloody confrontation took place at the end of 1681, and ended in heavy losses on both sides and in the weakening of Aurangzeb, who now had to face problems on other fronts. Since 1659 the Marathas of Maharashtra had organized under the leadership of a

Aurangzeb (above) took a simple, pious and austere approach to life. Preferring military campaigns to the comfort of life at court, he did not encourage artistic expression. During his reign, a great number of artists left the imperial studios to seek asylum in the courts of Rajasthan and Bengal. Unlike his predecessors, he was not much concerned with his appearance, and wore almost no adornments, apart from his sword (similar to the one on the left). He often fasted and, as Jean-Baptiste Tavernier related, he took his asceticism so far that he slept on the floor, covered with a tiger skin.

charismatic young war leader, Shivaji (1630–80). The Marathas, Hindus who were descended from the peasant classes of southern India, regularly came to the assistance of the sultans of Ahmednagar and Bijapur when they were in conflict with the Mughals. After serving the sultan of Bijapur, Shivaji turned against him and built up a strong army that henceforth fought all Muslim authority: the sultans and the Mughals. As his power grew, he undertook several raids, the most striking of which was the sacking of the port of Surat in 1664. He terrified people and made a point of punishing any towns and villages that refused to show him obedience. After his death, in 1680, his son Shambhaji pursued his policies. Along with the Marathas, there were now other groups opposed to Mughal power: the Jat peasants of the Mathura region, and the Sikhs of the Punjab, whose guru Arjun had been executed by Jahangir.

Aurangzeb was passionately interested in religious literature, and knew the Koran by heart (opposite).

Son of a dignitary from Ahmednagar who had entered the service of the sultan of Bijapur, Shivaji (left) made his mark as a warrior. While still very young, he annexed the fortresses of the Maharashtra and was made leader of an army of infantry, and then of cavalry. He imposed Hinduism as the state religion and, in the face of Aurangzeb's orthodox Islam, became the protector of the Hindu opposition. As the undisputed chief of an autocracy, he divided his state into provinces administered by governors. Shivaji was a good administrator and a military genius. To avoid conscripting his subjects during conflicts, he preferred to levy a tax on the whole population – thirty per cent of revenue in money or assets – to maintain an army of Hindu mercenaries, Malabars of low caste, elephants and camels. The French who settled in Surat provided him with artillery. The Marathas were hostile to both the Mughals and the British.

The return to religious orthodoxy

Faced with an increasingly organized opposition (Hindu and Shiite), the emperor brought about a return to a more rigorous Sunnite Islam, and fought in its name.

From 1668 to 1669 he took different measures designed to 'bring together the law that was in force with the ideal extolled by Islamic law', and to re-establish a real distinction between Hindus and Muslims. Edicts were promulgated that prohibited the construction of Hindu temples or regulated music, dancing and the consumption of alcohol, while the emperor, in his own court rituals, abandoned Hindu customs that had been introduced by Akbar, like the emperor's daily presentation to the masses. The severest measure was the reimposition in 1679 of the *jizya*, a tax levied on non-Muslims.

The conquest of the Deccan

Aurangzeb's reign was in fact just one long series of battles and surrenders that – although they brought the empire to its peak at one point – brought destruction, disorder and decline.

From 1686 to 1687 Aurangzeb focused on the conquest of the Deccan and the destruction of Maratha power. He began by subjugating the sultanates of Bijapur and Golconda before confronting Shambhaji's troops in 1689. Having been taken prisoner, Shambhaji was executed and his son Shahuji was kept as a hostage to neutralize the Maratha armies. This was the high point in Aurangzeb's conquests, and for the first time Mughal domination stretched to the far south of the peninsula.

After the destruction of the forts of Bijapur and Golconda, nothing remained of Muslim culture in the south of India. Aurangzeb's relentless annihilation of all opposition favoured the emergence of factions that opposed the Mughals, and resulted in the ruin of the imperial treasury. Below: a Maratha fortress.

Since the Middle Ages, the West has dreamed of India. This fascination was fed by the fantastic tales brought back by travellers who, like Marco Polo, had merely glimpsed the country. In the 18th century India remained as mysterious and incomprehensible as ever. It was a mixture of every paradox: religious feeling alongside crude idols, despotism alongside wisdom, and the wealth of sovereigns contrasting with the poverty of the people. The European travellers recounted with wonder their visit to Aurangzeb's court, although it was known for the austerity of its customs…. Jean Thévenot, François Bernier or even Jean-Baptiste Tavernier missed no opportunity to mention the gold and precious stones of the Great Mughal. In 1701 the Elector of Saxony, Augustus II, ordered his goldsmith Melchior Dillinger to produce a folly depicting the Great Mughal's court, with 132 figures in enamelled gold (left). Presented on a stage of silver, this imaginary evocation of the splendour at Aurangzeb's court comprises 4909 diamonds, 160 rubies, 12 pearls and 2 cameos.

Nevertheless, the victory was deceptive, because the Marathas, far from beaten, took up arms even more determinedly and harassed the Great Mughal. Sometimes using force, sometimes a clumsy diplomacy, he spent the rest of his life trying to oust an enemy who had become elusive.

An empire that has run out of steam

Aurangzeb fell prey to attacks of languor, and died in February 1707. His final years had been sad and solitary. His austerity and his long military campaigns had prompted courtiers and artists to leave the court. The luxury and pomp for which the Great Mughal had previously been well known had disappeared. His faithful followers died one after the other.

At almost ninety years of age, the emperor suffered numerous setbacks: not only was the empire he had so ardently defended not the one of which his ancestors Timur, Babur and Akbar had dreamed, but his numerous campaigns had emptied the coffers of the treasury which his economic and administrative measures had managed to refill. Even Indian Islam was not what the old man had hoped. In banishing the Sufis, who were considered heretics, the Mughal left the stage clear for the ulemas, who, through their incompetence and sectarianism, destabilized this great empire by setting themselves up as administrators and decreeing measures

The rulers of the Adil Shah dynasty of Bijapur claimed to be of Turkish descent. Heir to the throne at fifteen, Adil Shah II (below) was threatened both by Aurangzeb, who considered him a usurper, and by the Marathas. Refusing confrontation, he preferred to take refuge in his harem in 1666.

In his southern capital, Aurangabad, Aurangzeb had a tomb built for his wife, Rabia Daurani (left). Inspired by the Taj Mahal, this mausoleum with its awkward proportions bears witness to a decline in architecture.

Aurangzeb's eldest son, Bahadur Shah I (below), was the governor of Kabul before seizing the throne. Here he is depicted in a half-length portrait, with the stylized features all the rage in the 18th century.

that were often unsuitable. It was only on his deathbed that Aurangzeb acknowledged his mistakes and asked his successors to seek inspiration from the liberal policies of his predecessors, and not from his.

The emancipation of the nobility and the break-up of the empire

With the death of Aurangzeb, eternal quarrels over succession emerged once again. A series of rulers came to power who were incapable of confronting the great wave of discontent that was then sweeping the empire. The brief reign of Bahadur Shah I (1707–12), who was too old to take decisions that would have enabled Mughal authority to assert itself again, did not break down the structures of state, but his numerous military campaigns absolutely exhausted the treasury, which was located in Agra; it could no longer cover the empire's military expenses. The nobility turned against him, no longer considering him as the state's guarantor.

The short-lived hold on power by Jahandar Shah (1712–3) underlined the uneasiness of the Mughal sovereigns. For the first time, an emperor relinquished absolute power to the benefit of his *wazir*, giving rise to differences between the policies of the sovereign and those of his minister.

While the latter tried to arrange a reconciliation with the Jats, the Marathas, the Sikhs and Rajputs, the emperor lost all interest in the administration of his empire and gave himself over to the pleasures of the court.

Under Farrukhsiyar (r. 1713–9), this loss of imperial authority brought a drop in revenues which, henceforth, were no longer collected in the name of the central power but on behalf of local potentates. As the imperial armies were no longer receiving money, the order that had been established by the first Mughal sovereigns, and which rested to a large degree on their military superiority, disintegrated.

This lack of unity encouraged the independence of the nobles, who, for the most part, were henceforth recruited from the families of Indian Muslims and no longer from the elite constituted by the Persians and Turks. Little by little, they liberated themselves and organized their own interests without taking account of the state structure.

The Persian Nadir Shah administers the fatal blow to the Mughal empire

In the reign of Muhammad Shah (1719–48) the disintegration of the Muslim community, emphasized by the quarrels between Sunnis and

Born to a modest family in the Khorasan, Nadir (left) was a petty thief who became a strong warrior. By helping the shah to drive the Afghans out of Persia, he became his right-hand man. On the emperor's death he took power and the title of Nadir Shah.

During the reign of Muhammad Shah (sitting on the left), artistic production took on a new lease of life. Although hampered by the intrigues of the nobles, the ruler tried to maintain a way of life at court that recalled the former pomp. Rather than attempt to restore imperial authority, he withdrew to his palace, where he encouraged painters. His long reign marked the final stage in the empire's deterioration.

The Peacock Throne (above), made at the request of Shah Jahan, comprised a kind of platform resting on four golden feet and topped by an enamelled canopy. Above there stood a peacock with a golden body inlaid with precious stones. A ruby adorned its breast, from which hung a pear-shaped pearl. The bird's tail-feathers were made of sapphires and coloured stones.

Shiites, together with the rise in power of regional opposition groups, encouraged the invasion of the Persians on the orders of Nadir Shah in 1739. The latter, who had already imposed himself on the dynasty of the Safavids, was aware of the fragility of Mughal power, and decided to embark upon the conquest of India.

Having arrived in Delhi, his army had to subdue the popular revolts, and ended by pillaging the city. Two months later, Nadir Shah went back to Persia, taking the treasure of the Mughals, including the famous Peacock Throne, and striking the final blow to the declining dynasty. The Afghans took advantage of the situation to harass the Mughals on another front, and to take back the north-western provinces from them: Punjab, Kashmir and Multan.

After the sacking of Delhi, Muhammad Shah and his successors were completely incapable of confronting the rise of Indian and foreign powers. The sovereigns were men of little personality, more inclined to pleasure than the restoration of an empire. Because of their lack of interest in governing, they became puppets of their ministers, subject to the ambitions of different factions.

The principalities become autonomous, and the nawabs emerge

In 1708 the Rajputs took advantage of the weakening of the empire to rebel once again. The rajah of Jodhpur, dethroned by Aurangzeb, took back his kingdom and drove out the Mughal civil servants. When the rajah of Amber also showed a desire to revolt, the emperor Bahadur Shah I sent an army and subdued the rebellion. In 1709 the two rebels were reintegrated into the ranks of Mughal nobility. Being incapable of uniting, and totally reliant on the Mughal state structure and model, the Rajputs could not manage to organize their independence. However, they expanded their kingdoms by administering lands near their capital in the name of the Mughals. The empire, being in difficulties, diminished its control, and, little by little, the rajahs stopped paying

In Bengal, the state of Murshidabad began to prosper after Murshid Quli Khan took over the post of governor and administrator of taxes. Alivardi Khan (below), who succeeded in driving back repeated raids by the Marathas, was the last nawab to exercise his authority before the arrival of the British in Bengal.

their tribute to the imperial power. Yet their absence of cohesion and their internal dissensions prevented them from confirming themselves as one of the groups fighting over the remains of the empire.

In the north of India, the Sikhs, whose religion had always been recognized by the Mughals, remained on their guard. Their new guru, Govind Singh (1666–1708), who had supported Bahadur Shah I during the war of succession, was assassinated by the governor of the Deccan when he came to ask him for justice over the murder of his two sons by a Muslim noble. The designated heir, Banda (1670–1716), organized raids on Delhi and Lahore. Denigrated by certain opponents who disputed his title of guru, he was taken prisoner and executed in Delhi. Until the end of the 18th century and the reign of Ranjit Singh (1799–1839), the community, which was essentially established in the Punjab, organized itself into more or less clandestine cohorts.

The governors who were in charge of the oriental provinces for the Great Mughal – the nawabs, 'representatives' – took power in effect, and founded new dynasties. By refusing to be transferred regularly, as was formerly the custom in the

In 1797 Ranjit Singh (below), chief of one of the Sikh confederations, defeated the ruler of Afghanistan and demanded the title of maharajah of Lahore.

He then undertook the conquest of the local kingdoms and, by 1833, was head of an empire that dominated the whole of the Punjab. An opponent of British interests, he had attempted a short-lived alliance with Napoleon I and, recognizing the superiority of the European armies, had asked former soldiers of the French empire to form his own army. The British proposed a pact: they would not invade his kingdom if he broke off all relations with France. However, this agreement was short-lived. Just ten years after the death of Ranjit Singh, the British took over the Punjab.

Mughal empire, they succeeded in setting themselves up in their fiefs, in concentrating civil and military power in their own hands, in escaping the traditional division, and in ceasing payment of their tribute to the central power. However, despite their new independence, they did not break with Delhi.

Several states were founded in this way: Murshidabad on the Ganges became the capital of Bengal, taking the place of Dacca, which was too far away. Its founder, Murshid Quli Khan also obtained the government of the province of Orissa, and then that of Bihar. The state of Oudh in Bihar, the cradle of Shiism, was administered from 1739 by Safdar Jang, a minister of Muhammad Shah. His successors would regularly oppose the Maratha forces. In the South in 1715, Mubariz Khan became governor and diwan of Hyderabad. He succeeded in refusing to pay an annual tribute to the Marathas, thus declaring his independence. In 1724, he was killed by his enemy Nizam al-Mulk, a Sunnite opposed to the Persians, who created the famous dynasty of the Nizams.

The decline and fall of the Marathas

Since Shivaji, the Marathas had continually extended their influence. Being powerful in the Deccan, they threatened Mughal interests, and took advantage of the weakening of Delhi to demand the handing over of thirty-five per cent of the annual tribute that was paid by southern India. Although Bahadur Shah I accepted at first, Farrukhsiyar broke the pact and the Marathas made new forays. Under Muhammad Shah, they allied themselves with the Sayyid rebels, who opposed the emperor, to confront Mughal power. They managed to subdue the Deccan completely, and organized themselves into a powerful confederation. Their continual attacks enabled them to annex the provinces of Malwa, Gujarat and Bundelkhand, and to direct raids towards Delhi and the provinces of Punjab, Bengal, Orissa and Oudh. Since their only revenue was the booty seized from their enemies, their

After its defeat by the Afghans at Panipat in 1761, the Maratha confederation was greatly weakened. The heir, Madhu Rao, who was sixteen years old, could not have asserted his authority without the counsel of his minister, Nana Fadnavis (opposite, the young prince and his minister), and the support of Madhoji Scindhia (below). Later acknowledged as leader, the young ruler organized his government at Puna which, on his death, became the scene of revolts and intrigues. The British then tried to conquer the city, but were stopped by Madhoji Scindhia in 1779.

Madhoji Scindhia, chief of the Maratha clan of the same name established at Ujjain, began by supporting the legitimate heir Madhu Rao; then, in the name of the Maratha brotherhood, tried to seize the north of India. In 1771 he restored the Mughal emperor, Shah Alam II, to the throne of Delhi. In 1784 the emperor invested him with supreme power over Hindustan, but the different forces that dominated northern India opposed this nomination. Scindhia owed his life entirely to the battalions of the Frenchman de Boigne, who, at his request, had formed the first French brigade on Indian soil. Thanks to this army, he conquered his rivals in 1793, and expanded his power, but he died the following year in February before his ambitions could be realized.

power was solely reliant on their pillaging, as no other financial and economic structure had been solidly put in place. They were attracted by the wealth of the Punjab, and in 1757 joined the Sikhs to drive the descendant of the Afghans, Timur Shah, out of this region. Having won an annual tribute, a large part of the army withdrew and let Sikh power assert itself. Despite internal quarrels, through the extent of their territories they imposed themselves on 18th-century India as a great Hindu power that was determined to rip Muslim power apart once and for all.

When one of their chiefs was threatened in the north of the country by the Afghans, who tried to seize Delhi (where Shah Alam II was holding his ground), the Maratha troops gathered to confront the enemy. On 14 January 1761, at Panipat, the very place where Babur had formerly affirmed his power, the Maratha armies were completely decimated by the Afghan cavalry, which broke the impetus of this Hindu confederation.

The European presence expands

The settlement of the Portuguese in India, at the end of the 15th century, marked the start of an increasingly tangible European presence. From the 16th century British and Dutch vessels were trading in the different ports of India. In 1600, in order to take their share of the profits won by the Portuguese in the spice and cotton trade, British merchants joined together and created the East India Company. At about the same time, in 1602, the Dutch, who got their supplies of spices in Iberian ports, but were having their access to this supply blocked by Philip II, founded the Vereenigde Ooste Compagnie or V.O.C. They could now go and find spices at their places of production. Finally, it was under the aegis of Colbert that, in 1664, the Compagnie des Indes orientales françaises was created. Although a latecomer, the new company set itself up in certain Indian towns (Surat, Pondicherry) to obtain at a better price the merchandise which British and Dutch traders sold them at high rates. While the Dutch imposed themselves on the Indonesian islands, which produced nutmeg, cloves and pepper, the British set their heart on India, which not only enabled them to get supplies of various foodstuffs, but also opened up outlets for their domestic products. They set up their base at Gujarat, an important centre of textile production, and negotiated with the Mughal emperors to increase their concessions to the rest of India. In the 18th century, their policy of expansion was thwarted by French ambitions.

Indian craftsmen, especially weavers, worked in their villages. A merchant or *banian* took care of providing them with raw materials and selling their products. The Europeans dealt with these merchants in order to collect the produce that ships transported to Europe (above, embroiderers).

European interference in Indian conflicts

At the end of the 17th century the director of the East India Company, Josiah Child, advocated an extension of

British military power in order to establish a vast British dominion over India. Despite difficulties involved in the fact that the Compagnie des Indes was dependent on the wishes of the monarch and not on those of a coalition of merchants, the French also tried to increase their presence in India. Taking advantage of the collapse of the Mughal empire, both the British and the French fought for supremacy by interfering in the quarrels that opposed the different Indian forces.

The wars with the French in the south of the country prompted the British to increase their military strength by hiring native soldiers, sepoys. These armies moved towards Bengal to defend British interests, which were threatened by the local nawab. It was after this victory in 1757 at Plassey that the British general Robert Clive obtained the governorship of the provinces of Bengal, Orissa and Bihar from the emperor Shah Alam II (r. 1759–1806).

The nawab of Bengal sacked Calcutta, and many British were killed. Worried about the financial consequences that might result from an act of this kind, the East India Company recalled the British armies that were quartered in the South, commanded by General Robert Clive. They confronted the army of the nawab, who died on 23 June 1757 at the battle of Plassey, between Calcutta and Murshidabad. A new nawab, Mir Jafar, an ally of the British, was put in his place (below).

As the British progressed, the French, lacking the means and any true political will, became weaker.

Dupleix, the governor of Pondicherry, France's principal trading post in southern India, perfectly understood the kind of policy to follow in India, and had opposed the British advance by using Indian princes as intermediaries. However, in 1753 he was recalled to France, and abandoned India to British interests once and for all.

The Indian kingdoms, which had fallen prey to numerous internal disorders, did not seem to realize how the British were progressing. Only Tipu Sahib, sultan of the small state of Mysore, understood in 1782 that the British were on the way to annihilating them. He was killed, in 1799, at the battle of Srirangapatnam, where he confronted the British army for the second time.

From now on, recognized and powerful, the East India Company began a policy of territorial expansion under the leadership of Richard Wellesley, the governor general. To win its case, it offered subsidies to the different states that had been deprived of resources since the Mughal state structure had been broken up. In the face of fierce opposition, it imposed its authority by force. In 1818 the British armies annihilated the Marathas once and for all. From then on the East India Company,

The British presented Tipu Sahib (left), sultan of Mysore, as cruel and tyrannical, as well as a bigot. In fact Tipu Sahib was a cultured man, and also an astute military strategist who organized his army with the help of the French, who were better equipped than the Indians to fight his British enemies. Since he loved luxury and pleasures, he tried to make his court a place of refinement. He wore a round turban in the shape of a shield, which he decorated with two feathers of diamonds. Obsessed by his emblem the tiger, Tipu Sahib wanted all royal clothes and emblems to be decorated with stripes. He even went so far as to have an automaton made, representing a tiger devouring an British soldier. It was capable of producing both the roars of the beast and the groans of the man (below).

which was merely the instrument of the British crown, extended its power over the whole of the Indian subcontinent, with the exception of the Punjab, which was dominated by the Sikhs led by Ranjit Singh. On the latter's death, in 1839, his kingdom was split up, to the greatest benefit of the British, who finally managed to gain possession of it in 1849.

The last Mughals

After the short-lived reigns of Ahmad Shah Bahadur (1748–54), Alamgir II (1754–9), Shah Alam II tried

desperately to hold his ground. Having been blinded in 1788 by the Afghan chief Gulam Qadir, he was saved by the Maratha Sindhia. After 1803, the year in which the British took control of Delhi, all that remained by way of an empire for the emperors Akbar II (1806–37) and Bahadur Shah II (1837–58) was their shabby residence in Delhi's Red Fort, where they were allotted a home. A symbol of the durability of a once glorious empire, the Great Mughal was still officially recognized as the potentate. The British, who misunderstood Indian customs, feared that setting their own economic and

• The throne-room, which contained the famous peacock throne of emeralds and gold, is entirely white and gold. In some of the rooms the tall marble walls are strewn with bouquets of roses, roses like the roses of a Chinese embroidery, with tints varying from bright to pale pink, and whose every petal is faintly edged with gold. In other rooms there are blue flowers of lapis and of turquoise. Each room generally opens into the adjoining one.... Whirlwinds of dead leaves invade the silent palace and the white pavement where the precious throne once stood.•
Pierre Loti, *India*, trans. George Inman, 1906

political structures in place would provoke disturbances; so they maintained the authority of the puppet dynast to legitimize their presence. This was a clever manoeuvre but it backfired on them in 1857, during the Sepoy Rebellion, the revolt of the troops they had recruited among the Hindus and Muslims.

A cultivated man and a great poet, the last Mughal emperor, Bahadur Shah II, whom the sepoys had tried to restore to sovereignty (above, the confrontation with the British troops), died miserably in exile at Rangoon (now Yangon) in 1862 (opposite).

Page 128: the Red Fort of Delhi.

Two incidents caused the revolt to break out: the threat of sending the troops overseas to serve Britain, and the bringing into service of a new rifle lubricated with pork or cow fat, substances considered impure by both religions. In order to counter British power, the sepoys proclaimed Bahadur Shah II emperor of Hindustan. North India rose up, but, after the mutiny at Meerut near Delhi, on 9 and 10 May 1857, the British

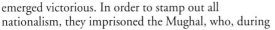

emerged victorious. In order to stamp out all nationalism, they imprisoned the Mughal, who, during the disturbances, had made himself the arbitrator between Hindu and Muslim sepoys. Arrested in September 1857, Bahadur Shah II was accused of disruption, treason and rebellion. While his descendants were executed, he was condemned to exile in Burma. The Mughal empire was swept away once and for all.

In order to impose the image of a sovereign on the Indians, the British wanted to name Queen Victoria empress of India. One section of Parliament was opposed to this, and it was only in 1877, at a durbar in Delhi, that Victoria (above), who was not present at the ceremony, was confirmed as empress of India.

After the seizure of Bengal by the British, Calcutta – future capital of the 'Raj' (a term designating the British government in India before 1947) – gained a wealth of new buildings: the William fort with the Maiden (promenade) laid out in cleared jungle, the Raj Bhawan (left), a financial and architectural folly commissioned by the governor general, Richard Wellesley.

DOCUMENTS

'Amongst the distant plains white cupolas, of that diaphanous pearliness that no artifice can ever imitate, are seen rising from the dusty haze that covers all the land, a haze which turns from blue to purple in the evening twilight.'

Pierre Loti
India, translated by George Inman, 1906

Emperors' memoirs

Written in the 16th century, the Babur-nama *was the first in a series of testimonies to the conquest of India. Autobiographical, like the memoirs of Babur and Jahangir, or written by relations, like the book of Humayun, these are precious documents concerning the life of the Mughal emperors.*

F lora and fauna of India in the *Babur-nama*.

India, a not very hospitable country

India had been given by Timur as an inheritance to his grandson, Muhammad, ancestor of Babur – hence the legitimacy that the latter claimed for its conquest. However, faced with this country's inhospitable nature, the first Mughal emperor hesitated to settle there.

Hindustan is a country of few charms. Its people have no good looks; of social intercourse, paying and receiving visits there is none; of genius and capacity none; of manners none; in handicraft and work there is no form or symmetry, method or quality; there are no good horses, no good dogs, no grapes, musk-melons or first-rate fruits, no ice or cold water, no good bread or cooked food in the *bazars*, no hot-baths, no colleges, no candles, torches or candlesticks.

   In place of candle and torch they have a great dirty gang they call lamp-men (*diwati*), who in the left hand hold a smallish wooden tripod to one corner of which a thing like the top of a candlestick is fixed, having a wick in it about as thick as the thumb. In the right hand they hold a gourd, through a narrow slit made in which oil is let trickle in a thin thread when the wick needs it. Great people keep a hundred or two of these lamp-men. This is the Hindustan substitute for lamps and candlesticks! If their rulers and begs have work at night needing candles, these dirty lamp-men bring these lamps, go close up and there stand.

   Except their large rivers and their standing-waters which flow in ravines or hollows (there are no waters). There are no running-waters in their gardens or residences (*'imaratlar*). These residences have no charm, air (*hawa*), regularity or symmetry.

   Peasants and people of low standing

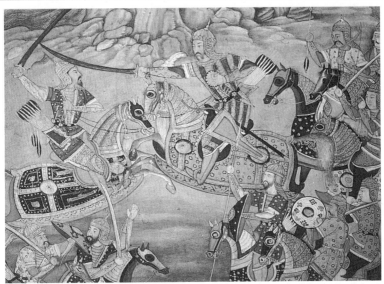

Battle of Rabat-i-Ruzak, in the *Babur-nama*: 'Tambal chopped so violently at my head that it lost all feeling under the blow.' (Translated by A. S. Beveridge, Vol I, 1922.)

go about naked. They tie on a thing called *lunguta*, a decency-clout which hangs two spans below the navel. From the tie of this pendant decency-clout, another clout is passed between the thighs and made fast behind. Women also tie on a cloth (*lang*), one-half of which goes round the waist, the other is thrown over the head....

Babur's army and India's climate

Babur's memoirs relate his army's difficulties in adapting to India.

It was the hot-season when we came to Agra. All the inhabitants (*khalaiq*) had run away in terror. Neither grain for ourselves nor corn for our horses was to be had. The villages, out of hostility and hatred to us, had taken to thieving and highway-robbery; there was no moving on the roads. There had been no chance since the treasure was distributed to send men in strength into the parganas and elsewhere. Moreover the year was a very hot one; violent pestilential winds struck people down in heaps together; masses began to die off.

On these accounts the greater part of the begs and best braves became unwilling to stay in Hindustan, indeed set their faces for leaving it. It is no reproach to old and experienced begs if they speak of such matters; even if they do so, this man (Babur) has enough sense and reason to get at what is honest or what is mutinous in their representations, to distinguish between loss and gain. But as this man had seen his task whole, for himself, when he resolved on it, what taste was there in their reiterating that things should be done differently? What recommends the expression of distasteful opinions by men of little standing (*kichik karim*)? Here is a curious thing: This last time of our riding out from Kabul, a few men of little standing had just been made begs; what I looked for from them was that if I went through fire and water and came out again, they would have gone in with me unhesitatingly, and with me have come out, that wherever I went, there at my side would they be – not that they would speak against my fixed purpose, not that they would turn back from any task or great affair on which, all counselling, all consenting, we had resolved, so long as that counsel was not abandoned. Badly as these new begs behaved, Secretary Ahmadi and Treasurer Wali behaved still worse. Khwaja Kalan had done well in the march out from Kabul, in Ibrahim's defeat and until Agra was occupied: he had spoken bold words and shewn ambitious views. But a few days after the capture of Agra, all his views changed – the one zealous for departure at any price was Khwaja Kalan.

When I knew of this unsteadiness amongst (my) people, I summoned all the begs and took counsel. Said I, 'There is no supremacy and grip on the world without means and resources: without lands and retainers sovereignty and command (*padshahliq u amirliq*) are impossible. By the labours of several years, by encountering hardship, by long travel, by flinging myself and the army into battle, and by deadly slaughter, we, through God's grace, beat these masses of enemies in order that we might take their broad lands. And now what force compels us, what necessity has arisen that we should, without cause, abandon countries taken at such risk of life? Was it for us to remain in Kabul, the sport of harsh poverty? Henceforth, let no well-

wisher of mine speak of such things! But let not those turn back from going who, weak in strong persistence, have set their faces to depart!' By these words, which recalled just and reasonable views to their minds, I made them, willy-nilly, quit their fears.

The Babur-nama in English (Memoirs of Babur), translated by Annette Beveridge, Vol II, 1922

The chronicle of Humayun

It was a Mughal princess, Gul-Badan Begam, daughter of Babur and sister of Humayun, who wrote this chronicle of Humayun's reign. After considering part of Babur's reign, she turns to Humayun's birth and accession to power, when Babur gives him the better part of the empire.

The blessed birth of the Emperor Humayun, the first-born son of his Majesty *Firdaus-makani*, occurred in the night of Tuesday, Zu'lqa'da 4th, 913H.

A banquet in a garden, a 17th-century miniature.

(6 March 1508), in the citadel of Kabul, and when the sun was in the sign of Pisces....

On Friday, Rajab 8th, 932 H. (20 April 1526) he [Babur] arrayed battle at Panipat against Sultan Ibrahim, son of Sultan Sikandar, son of Bahlul Lodi. By God's grace he was victorious, and Sultan Ibrahim was killed in the fight.... The treasures of five kingdoms fell into his hands. He gave everything away....

The Emperor made gifts in Agra to his Majesty Humayun and to all the mirzas and sultans and amirs. He sent letters in all directions, urgently saying, 'We shall take into full favour all who enter our service, and especially such as served our father and grandfather and ancestors. If such will come to us, they will receive fitting benefits.... The most High has given us sovereignty in Hindustan; let them come that we may see prosperity together.'...

A few days later he made an excursion to the Goldscattering Garden (*Bagh-i-zar-afshan*). There was a place in it for ablution before prayers. When he saw it, he said: 'My heart is bowed down by ruling and reigning; I will retire to this garden.... I will make over the kingdom to Humayun....

'Although I have other sons, I love none as I love ... Humayun. I crave that this cherished child may have his heart's desire and live long and I desire the kingdom for him and not for the others, because he has not his equal in distinction.'... That very day he fell ill, and Humayun poured water on his head, and came out and gave audience....

Next day he called his chiefs together and spoke in this wise: 'For years it has been in my heart to make over my throne to Humayun Mirza and to retire to the Goldscattering Garden. By the Divine grace I have obtained all things

but the fulfilment of this wish in health of body. Now, when illness has laid me low, I charge you all to acknowledge Humayun in my stead. Fail not in loyalty to him. Be of one heart and one mind with him. I hope to God that Humayun also will bear himself well towards men.

'Moreover, Humayun, I commit to God's keeping you and your brothers and all my kinsfolk and your people and my people; and all of these I confide to you.'...

Three days later he passed from this transitory world to the eternal home.

Gul-Badan Begam
Humayun-nama (The History of Humayun), translated by Annette S. Beveridge, 1902

Gul-Badan Begam was a natural at describing events, whether happy or tragic. After his exile in Persia, Humayun returned to India and had to cope with rivalry from his brothers.

When he [Humayun] crossed the pass, he sent *farmans* to summon Mirza Kamran and [cousin] Mirza Sulaiman and Mirza Askari, and said: 'We are on the march to fight the Uzbegs; now is the time for union and brotherliness. You ought to come as quickly as possible.' Mirza Sulaiman and Mirza Askari came and joined him. Then march by march they came to Balkh....

While Mirza Kamran was in Kulab, a woman named Tarkhan Bega, who was a thorough cheat, showed him the way by saying: 'Make a declaration of love to Haram Begam. Good will come of it.'

Acting on these words of an ill-judging adviser, he actually sent a letter and a kerchief to Haram Begam.... This woman laid the letter and the kerchief before the begam and then set forth the mirza's devotion and passion....

Portrait of Humayun.

In consequence of this affair, Mirza Sulaiman and Mirza Ibrahim were displeased with Mirza Kamran, or rather they became his enemies. They wrote to the Emperor that Mirza Kamran wished to thwart him and that this could not be better seen than in his failure to go to Balkh with him....

A year later word was brought that Mirza Kamran had collected troops and was preparing for war. His Majesty also, taking military appurtenances, set out for the mountain passes (*tangayha*) with Mirza Hindal....

In the fight on 20 November 1551, Hindal was killed.

His Majesty sent letters to his sisters in Kabul, and the city at once became like one house in mourning. Doors and walls ... wept and bewailed the death of the happy, martyred Mirza....

It was by Mirza Kamran's evil fate that Mirza Hindal became a martyr. From that time forth we never heard that his affairs prospered. On the contrary, they waned day by day and came to naught and perished. He set his face to evil in such a fashion that fortune never befriended him again nor gave him happiness. It was as though Mirza Hindal had been the life, or rather the light-giving eye of Mirza Kamran, for after that same defeat he fled....

Mirza Kamran is eventually captured and brought to the emperor, who is advised to kill him.

'This is no brother! This is your Majesty's foe!'... His Majesty answered: 'Though my head inclines to your words, my heart does not.'

Finally he is persuaded to go along with this course of action.

When he drew near to Rohtas, the emperor gave an order to Sayyid Muhammad: 'Blind Mirza Kamran in both eyes.' The sayyid went at once and did so.

Gul-Badan Begam
Humayun-nama (The History of Humayun), translated by Annette S. Beveridge, 1902

The diary of an emperor: the *Tuzuk-i-Jahangiri*

Like Babur, Jahangir took pains to write his memoirs. In this extract, he gives a description of Kashmir.

The merchants and artificers of this country are mostly Sunnis, while the soldiers are Imamiyya Shias. There is also the sect of Nur-bakhshis. There is also a body of Faqirs whom they call *Rishis*. Though they have not religious

Jahangir's tomb at Lahore.

maunds [1 maund = 37 kilos], placed one on the other. Near the city there is a small hill which they call Kuh-i-Maran (The Wicked Hill …), as well as Hari Parbat. On the east side of the hill there is the Dal Lake, which measures round a little more than 6½ koss [6 km long by 4 km wide or 3¾ miles long by 2½ wide]. My father (may the lights of Allah be his testimony!) gave an order that they should build in this place a very strong fort of stone and lime; this had been nearly completed during the reign of this suppliant, so that the little hill has been brought into the midst of the fortifications, and the wall of the fort built round it. The lake is close to the fort, and the palace overlooks the water. In the palace there was a little garden, with a small building in it in which my revered father used constantly to sit. At this period it appeared to me to be very much out of order and ruinous. As it was the place where that veritable *qibla* (place turned towards in prayer) and visible Deity used to sit, and it is really a place of prostration for this suppliant, therefore its neglected state did not appear right to me. I ordered Mu'tamid K., who is a servant who knows my temperament, to make every effort to put the little garden in order and repair the buildings. In a short space of time, through his great assiduity, it acquired new beauty. In the garden he put up a lofty terrace 32 yards square, in three divisions (*qit'a*), and having repaired the building he adorned it with pictures by masterhands, and so made it the envy of the picture gallery of China. I called this garden *Nur-afza* (light increasing).

Tuzuk-i-Jahangiri or Memoirs of Jahangir, translated by Alexander Rogers and edited by Henry Beveridge, Vol II, 1914

knowledge or learning of any sort, yet they possess simplicity, and are without pretence. They abuse no one, they restrain the tongue of desire, and the foot of seeking; they eat no flesh, they have no wives, and always plant fruit-bearing trees in the fields, so that men may benefit by them, themselves deriving no advantage. There are about 2000 of these people. There is also a body of brahmans living from of old in this country, who still remain there and talk in the Kashmiri tongue. Outwardly one cannot distinguish them from Mussulmans. They have, however, books in the Sanskrit language, and read them. They carry into practice whatever relates to the worship of idols. Sanskrit is a language in which the learned of India have composed books, and esteem them greatly. The lofty idol temples which were built before the manifestation of Islam are still in existence, and are all built of stones, which from foundation to roof are large, and weigh 30 or 40

India and the West

In the 17th century Mughal India had a sumptuous court that attracted travellers and ambassadors from every country. Thomas Roe, Jean-Baptiste Tavernier and François Bernier describe the luxury of the court.

An ambassador of James I of England is received at Jahangir's court

At the request of the East India Company in 1614, Thomas Roe was sent to India by James I to establish British interests. Here he is present at the emperor's birthday.

This day was the birth of the King and solemnized as a great feast, wherin the King is weighed against some jewells, gould, silver, stuffs of goulde [and?] silver, silke, butter, rice, frute, and many other things, of every sort a little, which is given to the *Bramini.* To this solemnitye the King commanded Asaph Chan [a dignitary and a son of the prime minister] to send for mee, who so doeing appoynted mee to come to the place wher the King sitts out at *durbarr,* and there I should bee sent for in. But the messenger mistaking, I went not untill *durbarr* tyme; and soe missed the sight. But being there before the King came out, as soone as hee spyed mee, hee sent to knowe the reason why I came not in, hee having geven order. I answered according to the error; but hee was extreame angry and chydd Asaph Chan publiquely. He was so rich in jewells that I must confesse I never saw togither so unvaluable wealth. The tyme was spent in bringing of his greatest eliphants before him, some of which, beeing lord eliphants, had their chaynes, bells, and furniture of gould and silver, attended with many guilt banners and flaggs, and eight or ten eliphants wayting on him, clothed in gould, silke, and silver. Thus passed about twelve companyes most richly furnished, the first having all the playtes on his head and breast sett with rubyes and emralds, beeing a beast of a woonderfull stature and beauty. They all bowed downe befor the King, making reverence very handsomly, and was a showe as woorthy as I ever saw any of beasts only. The keepers of every chefe eliphant gave a present. So, with gratious complements to mee, he rose and went in.

The diplomat is summoned to give the emperor a portrait, on which he is very keen....

At night about ten of the clock hee sent for mee. I was abedd. The message was: hee hard I had a picture which I had not showed him, desiering mee to come to him and bring yt; and if I would not give it him, yet that hee might see yt and take coppyes for his wives. I rose and carryed yt with mee. When I came in, I found him sitting crosse leggd on a little throne, all cladd in diamonds, pearles, and rubyes; before him a table of gould, on yt about 50 peeces of gould plate, sett all with stones, some very great and extreamly rich, some of lesse valew, but all of them almost covered with small stones; his nobilitye about him in their best equipage, whom hee commanded to drinck froliquely, severall wynes standing by in great flagons. When I came neare him, hee asked for the picture. I showed him two. Hee seemed astonished at one of them; and demanded whose it was. I answered a frend of myne that was dead. Hee asked mee if I would give it him. I replyed that I esteemed it more then any thing I possessed, because it was the image of one that I loved dearly and could never recover: but that if His Majestie would pardon mee my fancy and accept of the other, which was a French picture but excellent woorke, I would most willingly give it him. Hee sent me thancks, but that it was that only picture hee desired, and loved as well as I, and that, if I would give it him, hee would better esteeme of it then the richest jewell in his house.

J ahangir receives an artist.

Later on Thomas Roe describes the interview between Jahangir and the Persian ambassador.

Here first the Persian embassador saluted me, with a silent complement only. In the middst of this court was a throwne of mother of pearle borne on two pillars raysed on earth, covered over with an high tent, the pole headed with a knob of gould; under it canopyes of cloth of gould; under foote carpetts. When the King came neare the doore, some noble men came in and the Persian ambassador. Wee stood one of the one syde, the other of the other, making a little lane. The King entering cast his eye on mee, and I made a reverence; hee layd his hand on his brest and bowed, and turning to the other syde nodded to the Persian. I followed at his heeles till hee ascended, and every man cryed 'Good joy and fortune', and so tooke our places. Hee called for water, washed his hands, and departed. His weomen entered some other port [i.e. gate or entrance] to their quarter, and his sonne I saw not. Within this whole rayle was about 30 divisions with tents. All the noble men retired to theirs, which were in excellent formes, some all white, some greene, some mingled; all encompassd as orderly as any house; one of the greatest raretyes and magnificencyes I ever saw. The vale showed like a bewtifull citty, for that the raggs nor baggage were not mingled. I was unfitted with carriadge, and ashamed of my provision; but five years allowance would not have furnished mee with one indifferent sute sortable to others. And, which adds to the greatnes, every man hath a double, for that one goes before to the next remoove and is sett a day before the King riseth from these. So I returned to my poore house.

The Embassy of Sir Thomas Roe to India 1615–9, edited by William Foster, 1926

An adventurous Frenchman

The most assiduous of the European travellers were the jewellers, attracted to India by the possibilities of trading in precious stones. Of Augustin Hiriart, it is known that he originated in Bordeaux, and that he frequented Jahangir's court at Lahore. According to Tavernier, he was probably killed by poisoning. This letter is transcribed from an unpublished manuscript.

I have been in this country for eight years, and all the French I brought with me died; afterwards I entered the service of the Great Mughal King, who gave me four écus per day and one hundred and twenty per year.... Last year he made me captain of two hundred horses; I made him a royal throne in which there are not only several millions in gold and silver but also several inventions such as a diamond of a hundred 'quilats' that took ten days to cut. The splendours of this king are scarcely to be believed: one might just mention three big diamonds, and as for balas rubies he has more than all the men in the world; and when he travels through his country he takes fifteen hundred thousand human beings, horsemen, soldiers, officers, women, children, with ten thousand elephants, and with a great deal of artillery even though it is of no use except through its grandeur. He gave me elephants, horses, a house, and his face in gold to hang from my hat, which is a sign of honour like the order of the Holy Spirit in France. I have married, I have a child of two; and yet I still have a ticklish desire to see my homeland again. One year from now I want to ask for permission to leave, and take an elephant with me. I pray you to send to the ambassador, if he can pass freely through Turkey and even the city of Ispahan, addressing the letter to the Padres Carmelitanos in Spain; they will send me the letter at the court of this Great Mughal king. I also pray you to give a commentary on this letter to Mr Castaviac, a merchant jeweller on the palace square in Bordeaux, so that my parents know that God has not yet taken the thread of my life.

With my humble recommendations, your servant Augustin Houaremand, a name that the king gave me in Persian, and which means inventor of the arts.

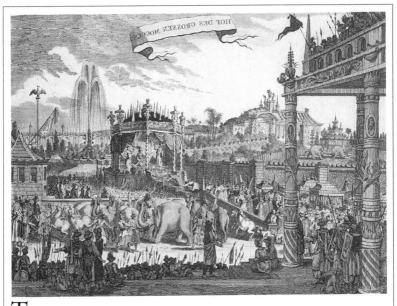

The Great Mughal's court, 18th-century German engraving.

A jeweller contemplates the riches of the Great Mughal

Jean-Baptiste Tavernier visited Turkey and Persia before reaching India in 1648. A diamond merchant, he was fascinated by the numerous jewels and precious stones of the Great Mughal. In his account, originally published in French in 1676, he describes the customs of Aurangzeb's court.

In which a certain Augustin de Bordeaux is mentioned....

All then that is remarkable at Agra is the palace of the King, and some beautiful tombs both near the town and in the environs. The palace of the King is a considerable enclosure with a double wall, which is terraced in some places, and above the wall small dwellings have been built for certain officers of the court. The Jumna flows in front of the palace; but between the wall and the river there is a large square where the King makes his elephants fight. They have purposely selected this spot near the water, because the elephant which has been victorious being enraged, they would not be able to pacify him for a long time if they did not urge him into the river, to effect which it is necessary to use artifice, by attaching to the end of a hand-pike fuses and petards, which are set on fire to drive him into the water; and when he is two or three feet deep in it he forthwith becomes appeased....

Shah Jahan had intended to cover the arch of a great gallery [with a trellis of rubies and emeralds] ... and a Frenchman, named Augustin de Bordeaux, was to have done the work. But the

Great Mogul [Mughal] seeing there was no one in his kingdom who was more capable to send to Goa to negotiate an affair with the Portuguese, the work was not done, for, as the ability of Augustin was feared, he was poisoned on his return from Cochin....

Since Aurangzeb, who reigns at present, has occupied the throne of the Moguls, which he usurped from his father and brothers, he has imposed on himself, as I have said, a severe form of penance, and eats nothing which has enjoyed life. As he lives upon vegetables and sweetmeats only, he has become thin and meagre, to which the great fasts which he keeps have contributed. During the whole of the duration of the comet of the year — [1665], which appeared very large in India, where I then was, Aurangzeb only drank a little water and ate a small quantity of millet bread; this so much affected his health that he nearly died, for besides this he slept on the ground, with only a tiger's skin over him, and since that time he has never had perfect health.

I remember having seen the King drink upon three different occasions while seated on his throne. He had brought to him upon a golden saucer, enriched with diamonds, rubies, and emeralds, a large cup of rock crystal, all round and smooth, the cover of which was of gold, with the same decoration as the saucer. As a rule no one sees the King eat except his womenkind and eunuchs, and it is very rarely that he goes to eat at the house of any of his subjects, whether of a Prince or even of his own relatives. While I was on my last journey, Zafar Khán, who was his *Grand Vizier*, and besides that his uncle on his wife's side, invited the King to visit him in order to see the new palace which he had had built for himself. This being the greatest honour his Majesty could do him, Zafar Khán and his wife, in testimony of their gratitude, made

him a present of jewels, elephants, camels, horses, and other things, to the value of seven *lakhs* of rupees (700,000) which amount to one million and fifty thousand (1,050,000) *livres* of our money [£78,750]. This wife of Zafar Khán is the most magnificent and the most liberal woman in the whole of India, and she alone expends more than all the wives and daughters of the King put together; it is on this account that her family is always in debt, although her husband is practically master of the whole Empire. She had ordered a grand banquet to be prepared for the King, but his Majesty, as he did not wish to eat at Zafar Khán's house, returned to the palace, and the Princess sent after him the dishes she had destined for him. The King found all the dishes so much to his taste that he gave 500 rupees to the eunuch who brought them, and double that amount to the kitchen....

Once a fortnight the King goes out to hunt, and while *en route* he is always mounted on his elephant, as also while the chase lasts. All the beasts which he shoots are driven within musket range of his elephant. Ordinarily these are lions, tigers, deer, and gazelles – for, as for wild boars, he as a good Muhammadan does not wish to see them. On his return he uses a *pallankeen*, and there is the same guard and the same order as when he goes to the mosque, save that at the chase there are 200 or 300 horsemen who ride before him in confused ranks.

As for the Princesses, whether they are the wives of the King, his daughters, or his sisters, they never leave the palace except when they go to the country for a few days' change of air and scene. Some of them go, but rarely, to visit the ladies of the nobles, as for example the wife of Zafar Khán, who is the King's aunt. This is not done except by the special permission of the King. It is not here as in Persia where the Princesses only make their visits at night, accompanied by a great number of eunuchs, who drive away all persons whom they meet on the road. But at the court of the Great Mogul the ladies generally go out at nine o'clock in the morning, and have only three or four eunuchs to accompany them, and ten or twelve female slaves who act as ladies of honour. The Princesses are carried in *pallankeens* covered with embroidered tapestries, and every *pallankeen* is followed by a

small carriage which can only contain one person. It is drawn by two men, and the wheels are not more than a foot in diameter. The object in taking these carriages is, that when the Princesses arrive at the houses they are going to visit, the men who carry the *pallankeens* are only allowed to go to the first gate, where the eunuchs compel them to retire, the Princesses then change into the carriages, and are drawn by the ladies of honour to the women's apartments. For, as I have elsewhere remarked, in the houses of the nobles the women's apartments are in the centre, and it is generally necessary to traverse two or three large courts and a garden or two before reaching them.

When these Princesses are married to nobles of the Court they become the rulers of their husbands, who, if they do not live as they desire, and do not act according to their commands, as they possess the power of approaching the King whenever they wish, they persuade him to do what they please, to the disadvantage of their husbands; most frequently asking for them to be deprived of their offices. As it is the custom that the firstborn succeeds to the throne, although he be the son of a slave, immediately that the Princesses of the King's harem become aware that there is one among them with child, they use all conceivable methods to make her have a miscarriage. When I was at Patna in the year 1666, Shaista Khán's surgeon, who is a half-caste (*mestiv*) Portuguese, assured me that the Princess, wife of Shaista Khán, in one month had caused miscarriages to eight women of his harem, not permitting any children but her own to survive.

Jean-Baptiste Tavernier
Travels in India, translated by V. Ball
Vol. I, 1889

A French doctor at the Great Mughal's court

In 1658 François Bernier, a French intellectual and secretary to a famous scholar, Pierre Gassendi, arrived in India. He practised as a doctor to Aurangzeb. The feast of the Mina Bazar seems to have caught his attention.

Delhi, 1 July 1663

Letter to Monsieur de la Mothe le Vayer

A whimsical kind of fair is sometimes held during these festivities in the *Mehale*, or royal seraglio: it is conducted by the handsomest and most engaging of the wives of the *Omrahs* and principal *Mansebdars*. The articles exhibited are beautiful brocades, rich embroideries of the newest fashion, turbans elegantly worked on cloth of gold, fine muslins worn by women of quality, and other articles of high price. These bewitching females act the part of traders, while the purchasers are the King, the *Begums* or Princesses, and other distinguished ladies of the *Seraglio*. If any *Omrah*'s wife happens to have a handsome daughter, she never fails to accompany her mother, that she may be seen by the King and become known to the *Begums*. The charm of this fair is the most ludicrous manner in which the King makes his bargains, frequently disputing for the value of a penny. He pretends that the good lady cannot possibly be in earnest, that the article is much too dear, that it is not equal to that he can find elsewhere, and that positively he will give no more than such a price. The woman, on the other hand, endeavours to sell to the best advantage, and when the King perseveres in offering what she considers too little money, high words frequently ensue, and she fearlessly tells

'As for the princesses, they never leave the palace.'

him that he is a worthless trader, a person ignorant of the value of merchandise; that her articles are too good for him, and that he had better go where he can suit himself better, and similar jocular expressions. The *Begums* betray, if possible, a still greater anxiety to be served cheaply; high words are heard on every side, and the loud and scurrilous quarrels of the sellers and buyers create a complete farce. But sooner or later they agree upon the price, the Princesses, as well as the King, buy right and left, pay in ready money, and often slip out of their hands, as if by accident, a few gold instead of silver *roupies*, intended as a compliment to the fair merchant or her pretty daughter. The present is received in the same unconscious manner, and the whole ends amidst witty jests and good-humour.

●A whimsical kind of fair ... is conducted by the handsomest and most engaging of the wives.... These bewitching females act the part of traders.●

Chah-Jehan [Shah Jahan] was fond of the sex and introduced fairs at every festival, though not always to the satisfaction of some of the *Omrahs*. He certainly transgressed the bounds of decency in admitting at those times into the seraglio singing and dancing girls called *Kenchens* (the gilded, the blooming), and in keeping them there for that purpose the whole night; they were not indeed the prostitutes seen in bazaars, but those of a more private and respectable class, who attend the grand weddings of *Omrahs* and *Mansebdars*, for the purpose of singing and dancing. Most of these *Kenchens* are handsome and well dressed, and sing to perfection; and their limbs being extremely supple, they dance with wonderful agility, and are always correct in regard to time; after all, however, they were but common women. It was not enough for *Chah-Jehan* that the *Kenchens* visited the fairs; when they came to him on the Wednesdays to pay their reverence at the *Am-Kas*, according to an ancient custom, he often detained them the whole night, and amused himself with their antics and follies. *Aureng-Zebe* [Aurangzeb] is more serious than his father; he forbids the *Kenchens* to enter the seraglio; but, complying with long established usage, does not object to their coming every Wednesday to the *Am-Kas*, where they make the *salam* from a certain distance, and then immediately retire.

François Bernier
Travels in the Mogul Empire
AD 1656–1668,
translated by Archibald Constable
1891

The decline of the Mughal empire

British domination leaves a semblance of power to the last of those who were the 'Great Mughals'. However, though the palaces shone with a thousand riches, sadness and melancholy could be read on the faces of the fallen emperors.

A durbar at Delhi in the 1830s. The crown prince is followed by the English Resident and the commander of the escort.

The impressions of a Frenchman received at the court of Akbar II

In March 1830, the naturalist Victor Jacquemont was offered a robe of honour by the Mughal emperor during a durbar at Delhi. The sovereign, who was consigned to the Red Fort by the English, aroused the Frenchman's pity.

Delhi, 10 March 1830
To M. Venceslas Jacquemont, Paris

My Dear Father,

…And lastly Delhi: Delhi is the most hospitable place in India. Do you know what almost happened to me this morning? I very nearly became the light of the world, the wisdom of the State, the ornament of the land, etc; but luckily I escaped with no worse than a scare. This is the explanation: it will make you laugh. The Great Mogul, Shah Mohammed Akbar Razi Badshah, to whom the political resident sent a petition that he might present me to His Majesty, graciously held a durbar so as to receive me. Having been escorted

to the audience by the resident with considerable pomp, including a regiment of infantry, a strong escort of cavalry, and an army of servants and attendants, the whole completed by a troop of richly caparisoned elephants, I paid my respects to the Emperor, who was gracious enough to confer upon me a *khilat*, or robe of honour, which was put on my back with great ceremony under the supervision of the prime minister; and disguised as a khaimakam, like Taddeo (do you remember *L'Italiana in Algeri*?), I made a second appearance at his court. Next, with his own imperial hands, the Emperor (and note, if you please, that he is descended in the direct line from Timur, or Tamerlane) attached a couple of jewelled ornaments to my hat (a grey one, previously dressed up by his vizier as a turban). During this imperial farce I kept a gloriously straight face, for there are no looking-glasses in the throne-room, and all I could see of my fancy dress were my two long black-trousered legs sticking out below my Turkish

dressing-gown. The Emperor enquired whether there was a King in France and whether English was spoken there. He had never seen a Frenchman, if I except General Perron, who was in charge of him when he was a prisoner among the Mahrattas; and he seemed to scrutinize with great attention the burlesque figure resulting from my not very solid five feet eight, with long hair, spectacles and my oriental rig-out over my black suit. At the end of half an hour he withdrew, and I retired with the resident in procession. The drums rolled out a salute as I passed along the ranks in my embroidered muslin dressing-gown. Why were you not there to rejoice in your offspring!

It goes without saying that I found Shah Mohammed Akbar Razi a venerable old gentleman and the most adorable of princes. But he really has a handsome face, a fine white beard and the expression of a man who has long suffered misfortune. The English have left him all the honours of his royal state and console him for the loss of his power with an annual pension of four

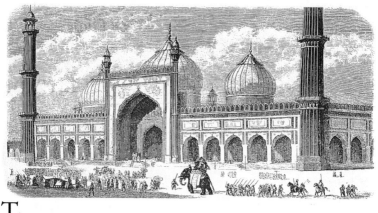

T he great mosque of Delhi, built in the reign of Shah Jahan.

million francs. Do not tell this story to those of my friends who are so fond of local colour, and at the carnival in 1833 or 1834 you shall see whether they do not consider my oriental disguise a very poor imitation: whereupon I will tell them what this poor imitation really is. The resident translated Victor Jacquemont, travelling naturalist, etc., by 'Mr. Jacquemont, Sahib Bahadurz', which means 'M. Jacquemont, lord victorious in war'. And that was how the grand master of ceremonies announced me.

Victor Jacquemont
Letters from India 1829–1832
Translated by Catherine Alison Phillips, 1936

Bahadur Shah II on the front page of *L'Illustration*

In the 19th century, the famous magazine L'Illustration *sent a journalist to India. He was received in Delhi by Bahadur Shah II. The text was published years later, when India became topical because of the Sepoy Rebellion.*

Delhi, 11 November 1842
I have been here for forty-eight hours. I had scarcely written to you, full of enthusiasm about the beauties of India, and especially its plains, when I entered an arid desert of dust, which lasted for several days: this was the approach to Delhi....

While I was out, I met the commander of the fort of the Great Mughal, an English captain whom I knew, and who offered me a lift in his 'buggy'. I got in, and, as we passed beneath the high walls of the Kreml of Delhi, walls of a kind of red marble (an ancient colour of red), we heard a far-off noise of kettledrums accompanied by other indistinct sounds. It was the royal cortege which was returning to the palace. 'Let's slip through here', he said to me, indicating a gigantic gate under which an elephant would have looked no bigger than a mouse, and with heavy doors in yellow copper with pointed nails. 'Let's slip through here into the first courtyard of the palace, and we'll see the procession.'

No sooner said than done, and we isolated ourselves under a tree with sprawling branches.

The noise of the drums and other instruments rapidly increased; but it was already almost dark when, two by two, entering through the Great Gate, crossing the courtyard and turning into another inside this immense enclosure. After these horsemen, who were pretty numerous, several litters and oxcarts passed by; then the crowd of musicians rushed through the gate into the courtyard, drawing from their instruments – trumpets, fifes and drums – all the sounds of which they were capable, and suddenly a bright torch-light enabled us to see a gaunt old man, with a severe countenance, sitting up straight in a sedan chair under a canopy. It was the Great Mughal. Twenty elephants followed immediately after him, any old how like a herd, some with gilt palanquins, others with drummers who weren't doing things by halves. In general, one must hand it to the Great Mughal's musicians, they really earn their pay; their zeal is like a kind of demoniacal frenzy.

After these elephants, so gloomy in appearance and with the sad, slow gait that characterizes these animals, there came some more horsemen, the stragglers, with immense *houkas*, flags, etc. Then all became silent once more.

I have not mentioned that the Great Mughal, seated on the sedan chair, held in his hand the hooked end of a gigantic *houka* which was carried behind him.

In the funereal light and the smoke of the torches he looked like an embalmed corpse, with the black colouring of a mummy, and adorned with glitter.'

A few days later, the traveller was presented to His Majesty, and had the chance to complete his portrait.

The fact is that the Mughal is a poor old man who can only put up with a ceremony by means of opium. He is then placed on the throne, and can only

'It was the Great Mughal. Twenty elephants followed immediately after him, any old how like a herd, some with gilt palanquins, others with drummers who weren't doing things by halves.'

remain there as long as the effect of the opium lasts.... The throne was a marble rostrum surrounded by a balustrade. In the middle of a splendid court, there was a vacuum around the monarch. A few old servants stood upright, shabbily dressed, with silver sticks. Two young boys, relatives of the emperor I suppose, were seated or rather half-lying at the foot of the throne.

The Mughal looked haggard. His eyes sometimes sparkled strangely, sometimes became as dull as tin; it seemed to me that he was trembling.... His clothes were made of velvet, in imitation of leopard-skin, and strangely decorated, in certain places, with strips of sable or other light furs. His face was gaunt, haggard and dark, as were his hands; he had a hook nose, and hollow cheeks; few or no teeth, a sparse beard dyed a reddish black that bordered on violet. On his eyes there was some black make-up.

This old man, whom I saw on the throne of Delhi, was Bahadur Shah, a descendant of Tamerlane.

'Voyages dans les Etats du Grand Mogol'
L'Illustration, 12 September 1857

The white splendour of the Great Mughals

A French navy officer, Julien Viaud (1850–1923), known by the name of Pierre Loti, travelled in India from 1899 to 1900. The articles he wrote for the 'Revue des Deux Mondes' were later published under the provocative title of L'Inde (sans les Anglais) *or* India (without the English).

Amongst the distant plains white cupolas, of that diaphanous pearliness that no artifice can ever imitate, are seen rising from the dusty haze that covers all the land, a haze which turns from blue to purple in the evening twilight.

These are the resting-places of the princesses who once trod these lofty terraces, and, arrayed in gold-striped muslins and precious stones, displayed their naked loveliness. The largest dome is that of the Taj, Taj the incomparable, where the great sultana, Montaz-i-Mahal [Mumtaz Mahal], sleeps since two hundred and seventy years ago. Everybody has seen and has described the Taj, which is known as one of the classic wonders of the world. Enamels and miniatures still preserve the features of the much-beloved Montaz-i-Mahal and of her husband, the sultan, who created the place, wishing to enshroud his dead wife with unheard-of splendour. Standing in a park-like cemetery that is walled in like a fortress, the Taj is the largest and most stainless mass of marble that the world has seen. The walls of this park and the high cupolas rising over the four outer gates are of red sandstone encrusted with alabaster, but the artificial lakes, shady groves, and boskages of palm and cypress that lie within display a cold formality of tracing. Out of these the incomparable monument towers forth in a whiteness which the surrounding sombre greenery seems to enhance. An immense cupola and four minarets, lofty as towers, stand on a white pediment, and everywhere the same restful purity of outline and the same calm and supremely simple harmony of tone pervade a colossal edifice entirely built of white marble, diapered by almost imperceptible lines of a pale grey. On coming nearer, delicate arabesques of thin black marble inlay are observed, which damascene the walls and underline the cornices, twining round the doors and minarets.

Under the central cupola, which is seventy-five feet [over twenty metres] high, the sultana sleeps. Here there is

•The largest and the most stainless mass of marble that the world has seen.•

nothing but the most superb simplicity, only a great white splendour. It should be dark here, but it is as light as if these whitenesses were self-illuminating, as if this great carved sky of marble had a vague transparence. There is nothing on the walls but veins of pearly grey and a few faintly outlined arches, and on the dome's white firmament nothing but those facets traced as with a compass, which imitate the crystal pendants of some stalactite cave. Around the pediment, however, there is a bordering of great lilies sculptured in bold relief. Their stalks seem to spring out of the ground, and the marble flowers look as if their petals were about to fall. This decoration, which flourished in India in the 17th century, has now been more or less indifferently imitated by our modern western art.

The wonder of wonders is the white grille that stands in the centre of the translucent hall and encloses the tomb of the sultana. It is made of plaques of marble placed upright, so finely worked that it might be thought that they were carved in ivory. On each marble upright and each stud with which these fretted marble plaques are surrounded little garlands of tulips, fuchsias, and immortelles are worked in mosaics of turquoise, topaz, porphyry, or lapis lazuli. The sonority of this white mausoleum is almost terrifying, for the echoes never seem to cease. If the name of Allah is intoned the exaggerated echo lasts for several seconds and then lingers in the air like the faint breath of an organ.... The throne-room, which contained the famous peacock throne of emeralds and gold, is entirely white and gold. In some of the rooms the tall marble walls are strewn with bouquets of roses, roses like the roses of a Chinese embroidery, with tints varying from bright to pale pink, and whose every petal is faintly edged with gold. In other rooms there are blue flowers of lapis and of turquoise.

Pierre Loti, *India*, translated by George Inman, 1906

CHRONOLOGY

INDIA BEFORE THE ARRIVAL OF THE MUGHALS

711–3 Conquest of Sind
998–1030 Mahmud of Ghazni invades India
1022 Founding of Lahore by Mahmud of Ghazni
1175–93 Conquest of Sind, the Punjab and Delhi by the armies of Muhammad of Ghor
1210–90 Slave dynasty
1290–1320 Khalji dynasty
1320–1414 Tughluq dynasty
1398 Invasion of India by Tamerlane
1414–50 Sayyid dynasty
1451–1526 Lodi dynasty
1498 The Portuguese at Calicut
1505 Founding of Agra by Sikandar Lodi

THE MUGHALS

1526 Babur's victory over Ibrahim Lodi at Panipat
1526–30 Reign of Babur over North India
1530–40 First reign of Humayun
1540–5 Reign of the Afghan Sher Shah
1555–6 Humayun returns to India
1556–1605 Reign of Akbar
1561–77 Expansion of the empire to Bengal, Rajasthan and Gujarat
1571 Founding of Fatehpur Sikri by Akbar
1572–80 Akbar undertakes important reforms
1585–98 Akbar at Lahore
1600 Creation of the East India Company
1602 Creation of the Dutch company Vereenigde Ooste Compagnie (V.O.C.)
1605–27 Reign of Jahangir
1611 Jahangir marries Nur Jahan
1628–58 Reign of Shah Jahan

1631 Death of Mumtaz Mahal
1632–52 Construction of the Taj Mahal
1635–6 Golconda and Bijapur become vassals of the Mughal empire
1639–48 Construction of Shajahanabad
1657–8 War of succession of Shah Jahan
1658–1707 Reign of Aurangzeb
1659–65 First attacks by Shivaji, leader of the Marathas
1664 Creation of the Compagnie des Indes orientales françaises
1679 Aurangzeb reimposes the *jizya*
1686–7 Subjugation of the sultanates of Bijapur and Golconda and destruction of their forts
1707–12 Reign of Bahadur Shah I
1710 The Sikh insurrection
1712–3 Reign of Jahandar Shah
1713–9 Reign of Farrukhsiyar
1719–48 Reign of Muhammad Shah
1742 Dupleix becomes governor of Pondicherry
1748–54 Reign of Ahmad Shah Bahadur
1754–9 Reign of Alamgir II
1757 Victory of the British at Plassey, Bengal
1758 The Sikhs become the masters of the Punjab
1759–1806 Reign of Shah Alam II
1761 Battle of Panipat, where the Marathas are crushed by the Afghans
1782–99 Tipu Sahib is sultan of Mysore
1799–1839 Ranjit Singh is ruler of the Punjab
1806–37 Reign of Akbar II
1837–58 Reign of Bahadur Shah II
1849 Annexation of the Punjab to the British crown
1857 Start of Sepoy Rebellion
1858 The East India Company is dissolved
1877 Queen Victoria proclaimed empress of India in Delhi

FURTHER READING

Abul Fazl, *The Ain-i-Akbari*, translated by Heinrich Blochmann, 1977
— *Akbar-nama*, translated by Henry Beveridge, 1897
Al-Badauni, *Muntakhabu't Tawarikh*, translated by William H. Lowe, 3 vols., 1884
Asher, Catherine B., *Architecture of Mughal India*, 1992
Babur, *The Babur-nama in English (Memoirs of Babur)*, translated by Annette Beveridge, 2 vols., 1922
Beach, Milo C., *Mughal and Rajput Painting*, 1992
Bernier, François, *Travels in the Mogul Empire*, translated by Archibald Constable, 1891
Brand, Michael, and Glenn D. Lowry, *Akbar's India: Art from the Mughal City of Victory*, 1985

Brown, Percy, *Indian Architecture: The Islamic Period*, vol. 2, 1952

Correia-Afonso, John, *Letters from the Mughal Court: The First Jesuit Mission to Akbar, 1580–1583*, 1981

Day, Upendra Nath, *The Mughal Government, AD 1556–1707*, 1969

Deloche, Jean, *Recherches sur les routes de l'Inde au temps des Mogols*, 2 vols., 1968

Frédéric, Louis, *Akbar, le Grand Moghol*, 1986

Gascoigne, Bamber, *The Great Moghuls*, 1987

Gul-Badan Begam, *Humayun-nama (The History of Humayun)*, translated by Annette Beveridge, 1902

Habib, Irfan, *An Atlas of the Mughal India*, 1982

Haudrère, Philippe, *La Compagnie française des Indes au XVIIIe siècle (1719–1795)*, 4 vols., 1984

Irvine, William, *Later Mughals*, 2 vols., 1922

Islam, Riazul, *Indo-Persian Relations: A Study of the Political and Diplomatic Relations between the Mughal Empire and Iran*, 1970

Jacquemont, Victor, *Letters from India 1829–1832*, translated by Catherine Alison Phillips, 1936

Kehren, Lucien, *Tamerlan, l'empire du seigneur de fer*, 1978

Koch, Ebba, *Mughal Architecture: An Outline of its History and Development (1526–1858)*, 1991

Markovits, Claude (ed.), *Histoire de l'Inde Moderne, 1480–1950*, 1994

Michell, George, and Antonio Martinelli, *The Royal Palaces of India*, 1994

Moreland, William Harrison, *India at the Death of Akbar, An Economic Essay*, 1920

Nath, R., *Private Life of the Mughals in India (1526–1803)*, 1994

Okada, Amina, *Imperial Mughal Painters: Indian Miniatures from the Sixteenth and Seventeenth Centuries*, 1991

Richards, John F., *The Mughal Empire*, 1993

Roe, Thomas, *The Embassy of Sir Thomas Roe to India 1615–19*, edited by William Foster, 1926

Roux, Jean-Paul, *Histoire des Grands Moghols*, 1986

Spear, Thomas George Percival, *Twilight of the Mughals: Studies in Late Mughal Delhi*, 1951

Tavernier, Jean-Baptiste, *Travels in India*, translated by V. Ball, 2 vols., 1889

Tuzuk-i-Jahangiri or Memoirs of Jahangir, translated by Alexander Rogers and edited by Henry Beveridge, 2 vols., 1909–14

LIST OF ILLUSTRATIONS

CHAPTER 2

CHAPTER 3

CHAPTER 4

INDEX

ACKNOWLEDGMENTS

The publishers thank Roland and Sabrina Michaud, both for their immense photographic library, which enabled most of this book to be illustrated, and for their invaluable advice. Grateful thanks also go to Jean Soustiel and Marianne Ganneau.

PHOTO CREDITS

TEXT CREDITS

Grateful acknowledgment is made for use of material from the following works:
(pp. 132–4) Gul-Badan Begam, *Humayun-nama (The History of Humayun)*, translated by Annette S. Beveridge, 1902; reprinted by permission of the Royal Asiatic Society, London. (pp. 136–8) *The Embassy of Sir Thomas Roe to India 1615–9*, edited by William Foster, 1926; by permission of Oxford University Press. (pp. 57 and 134–5) *Tuzuk-i-Jahangiri or Memoirs of Jahangir*, translated by Alexander Rogers and edited by Henry Beveridge, 2 vols., 1909–14; reprinted by permission of the Royal Asiatic Society, London.

Valérie Berinstain
is a lecturer in the history and civilization of India
at the Sorbonne and at the Institut national des
Langues et Civilisations orientales with a doctorate
in Indian studies and a diploma from the Ecole
du Louvre. Her research is primarily focused
on economic trade between India and Europe
from the 16th to the 19th centuries.
Her work has resulted in several publications,
including editing a previously unpublished
manuscript by a French merchant in India,
*Georges Roques: La manière de négocier aux Indes,
1676–1691, la Compagnie des Indes et l'art du
commerce*, 1996.

For Dadou

In memory of Maurice Berinstain, my grandfather

Translated from the French by Paul G. Bahn

For Harry N. Abrams, Inc.
Eve Sinaiko, editorial
Dana Sloan, cover design

Library of Congress Cataloging-in-Publication Data

Bérinstain, Valérie.
    [Inde impériale des grands Moghols. English]
    India and the Mughal dynasty / Valérie Bérinstain.
        p.   cm. — (Discoveries)
    Includes index.
    ISBN 0–8109–2856–6 (pbk.)
    1. Mogul Empire—History. 2. India—History—1526–1765. 3. Art—
Mogul.   I. Title.   II. Series: Discoveries (New York, N.Y.)
DS641.B47   1998
954.02'5—dc21   97–42423